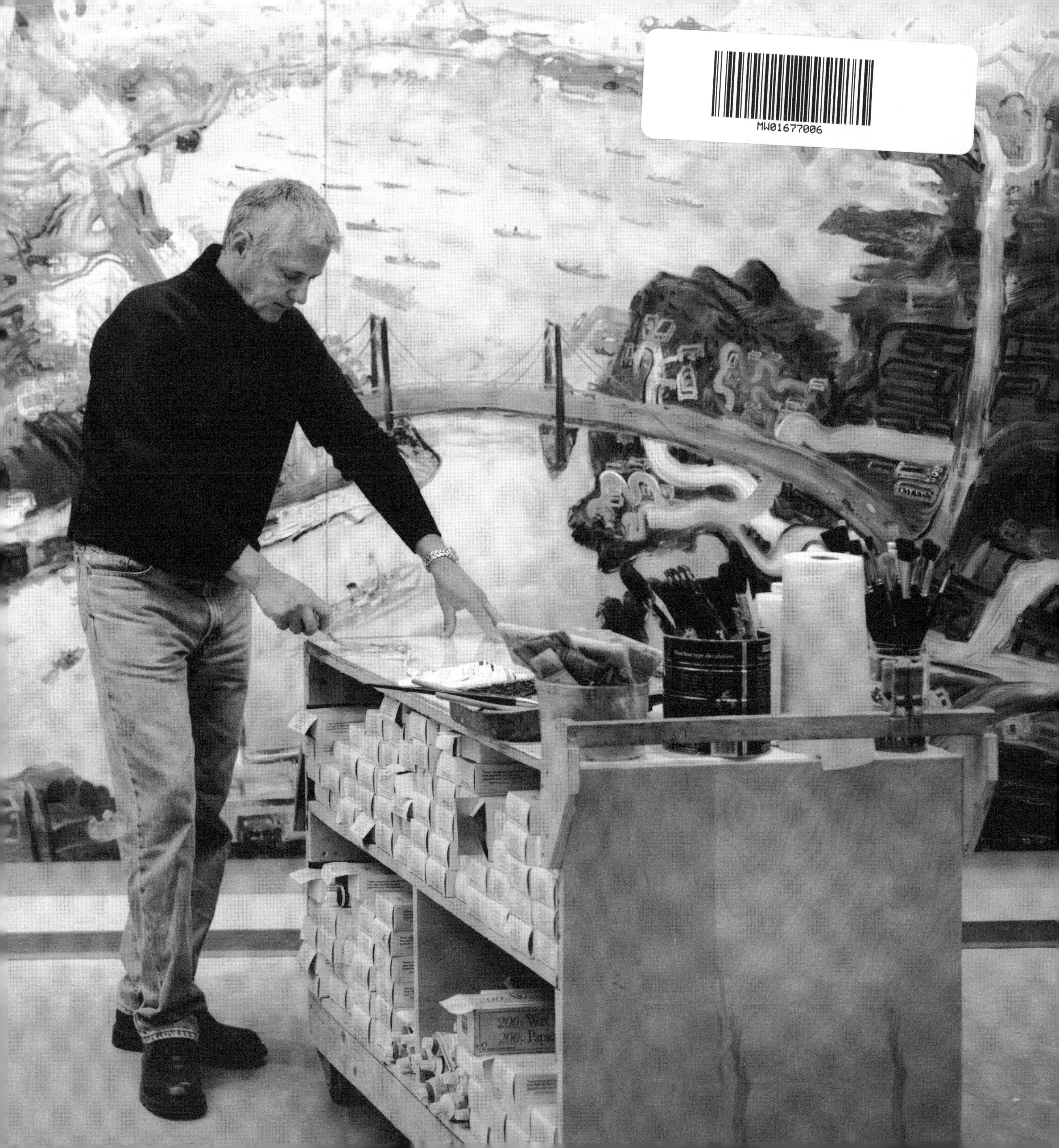

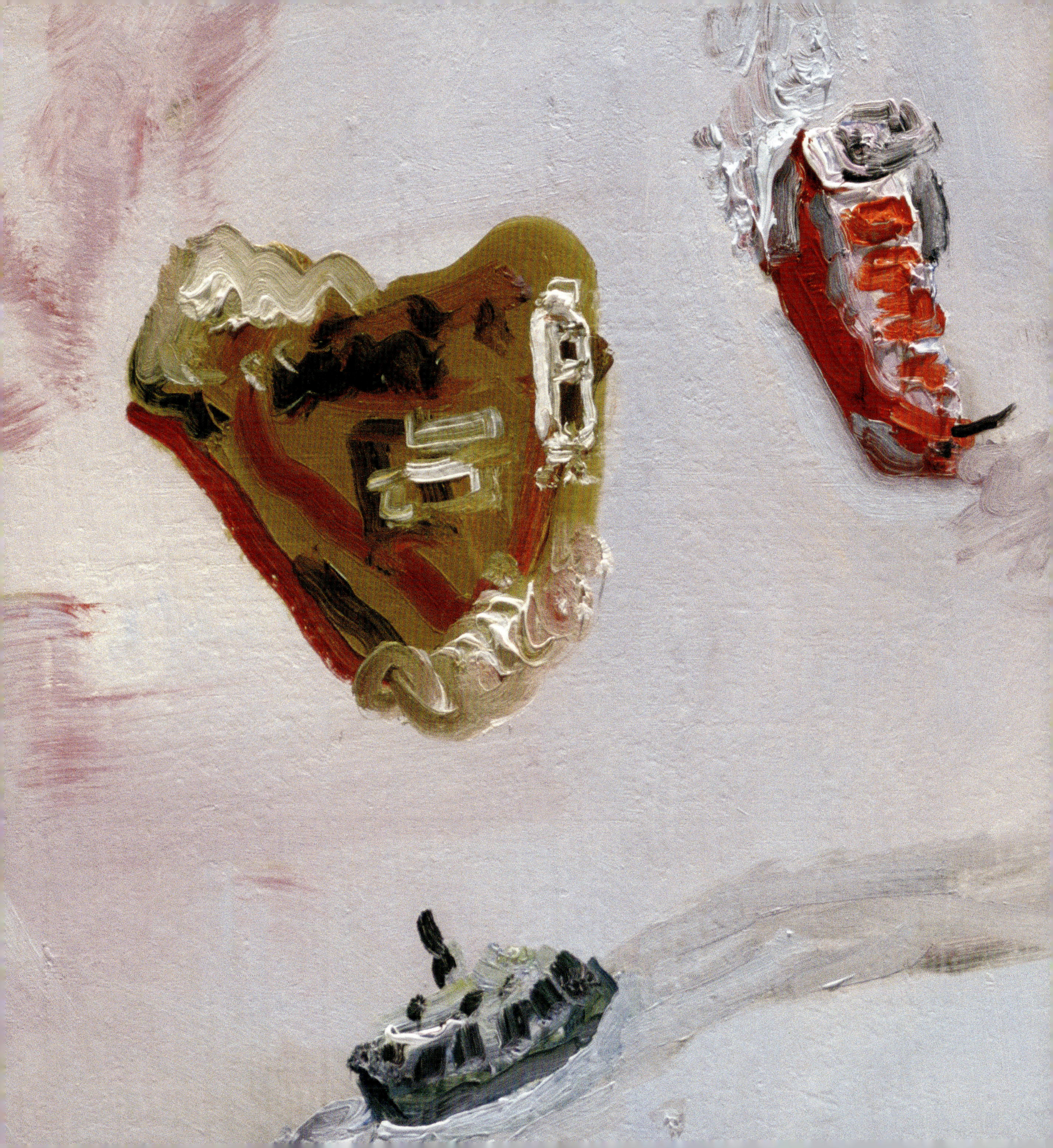

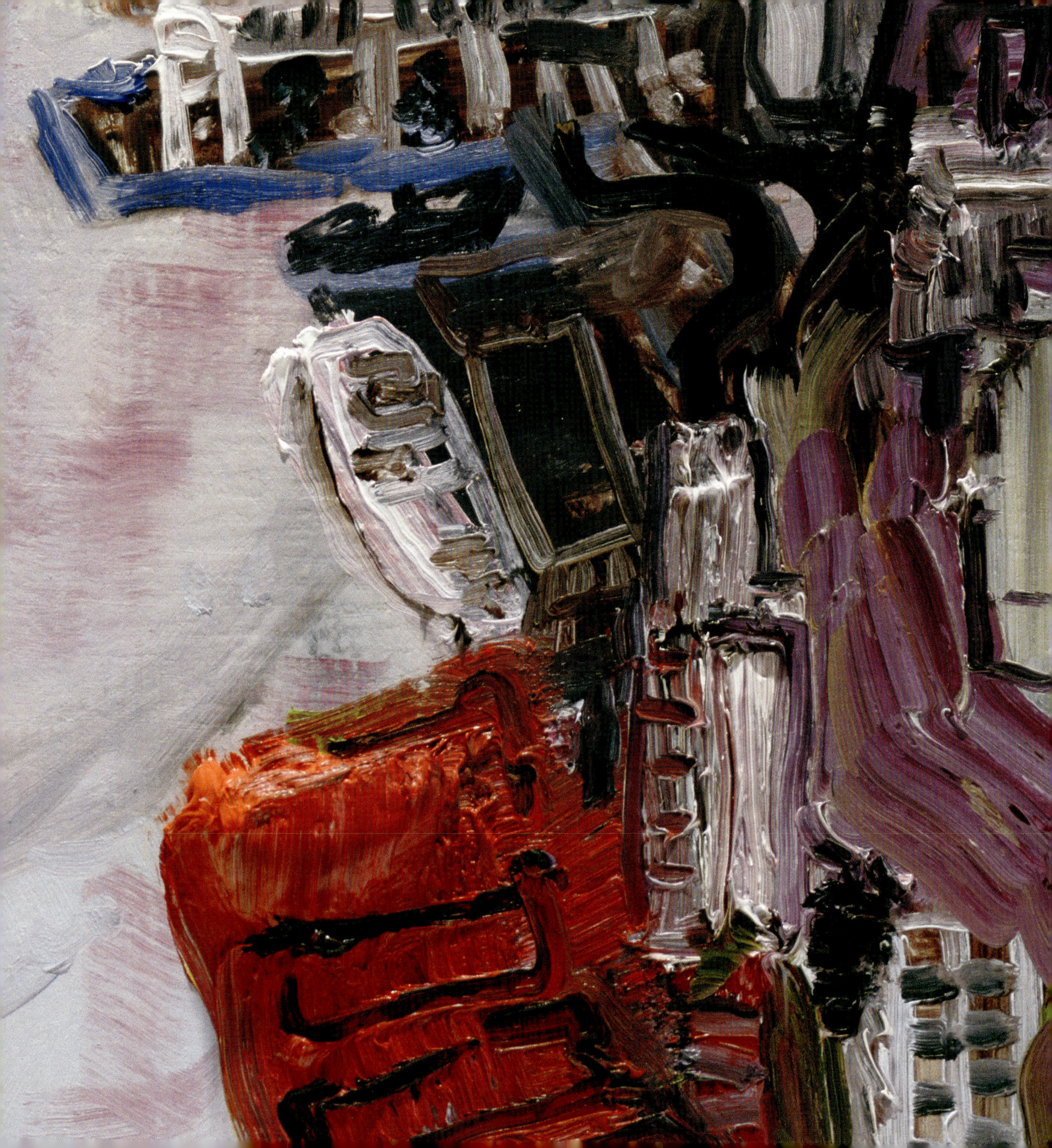

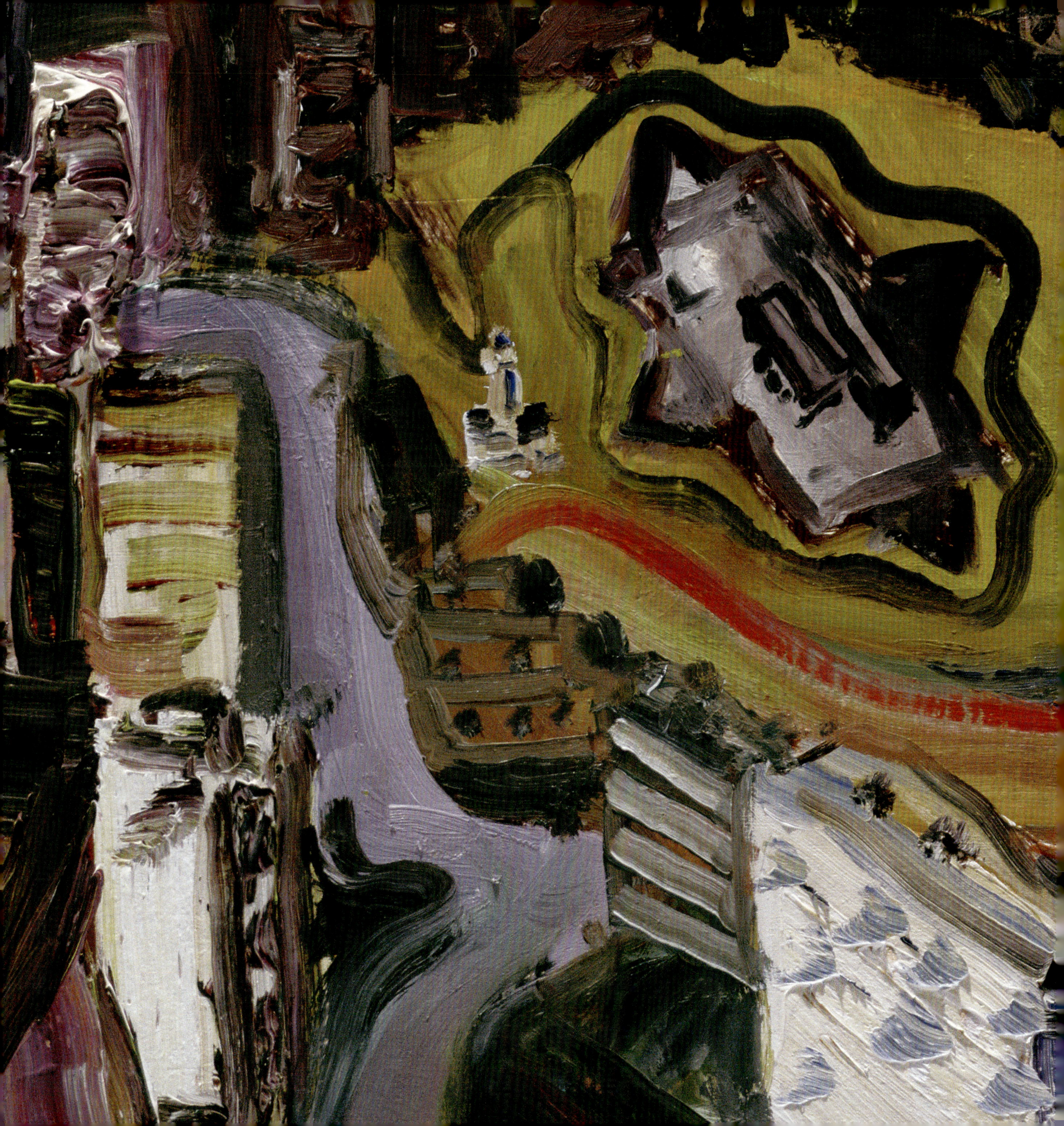

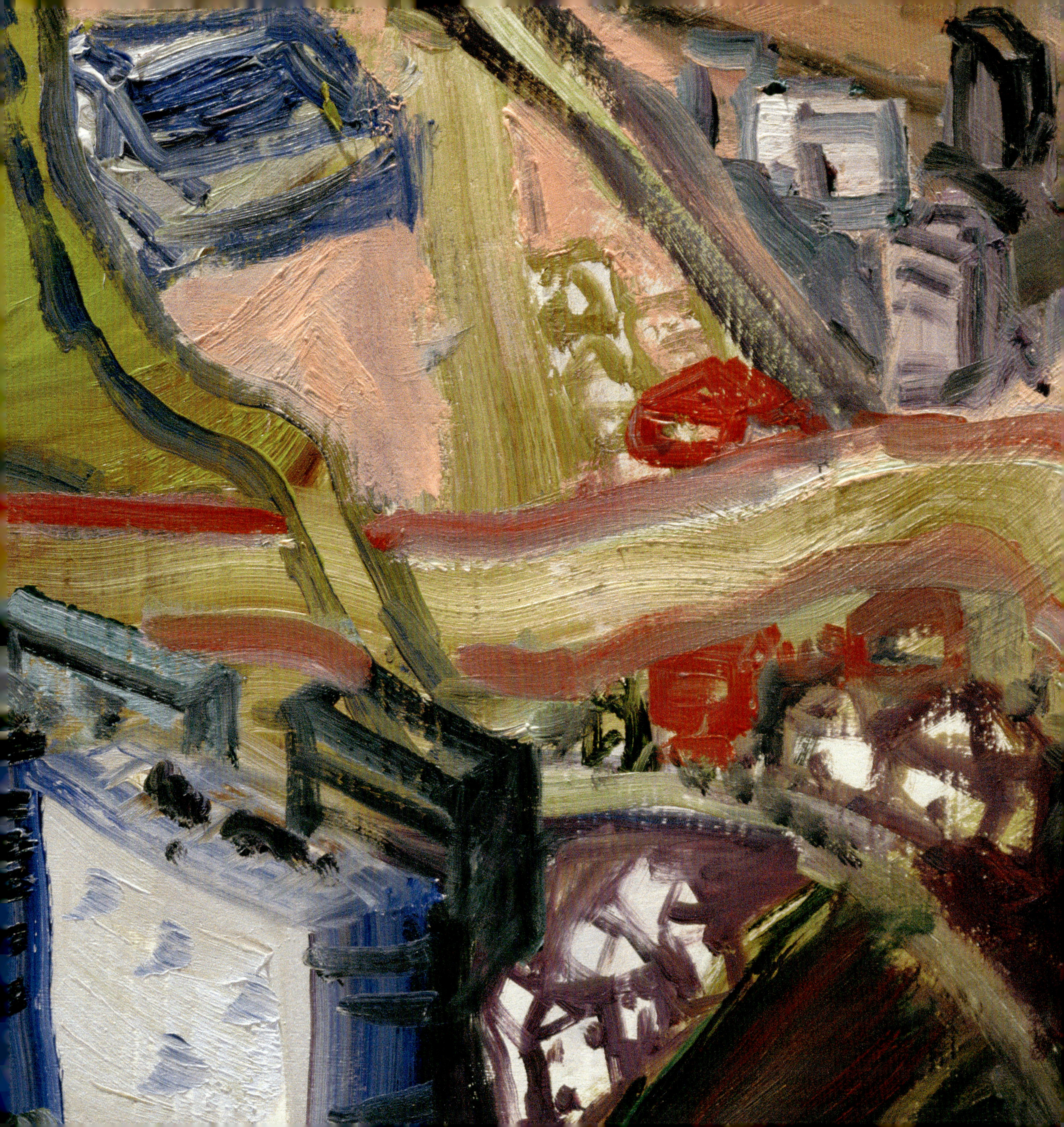

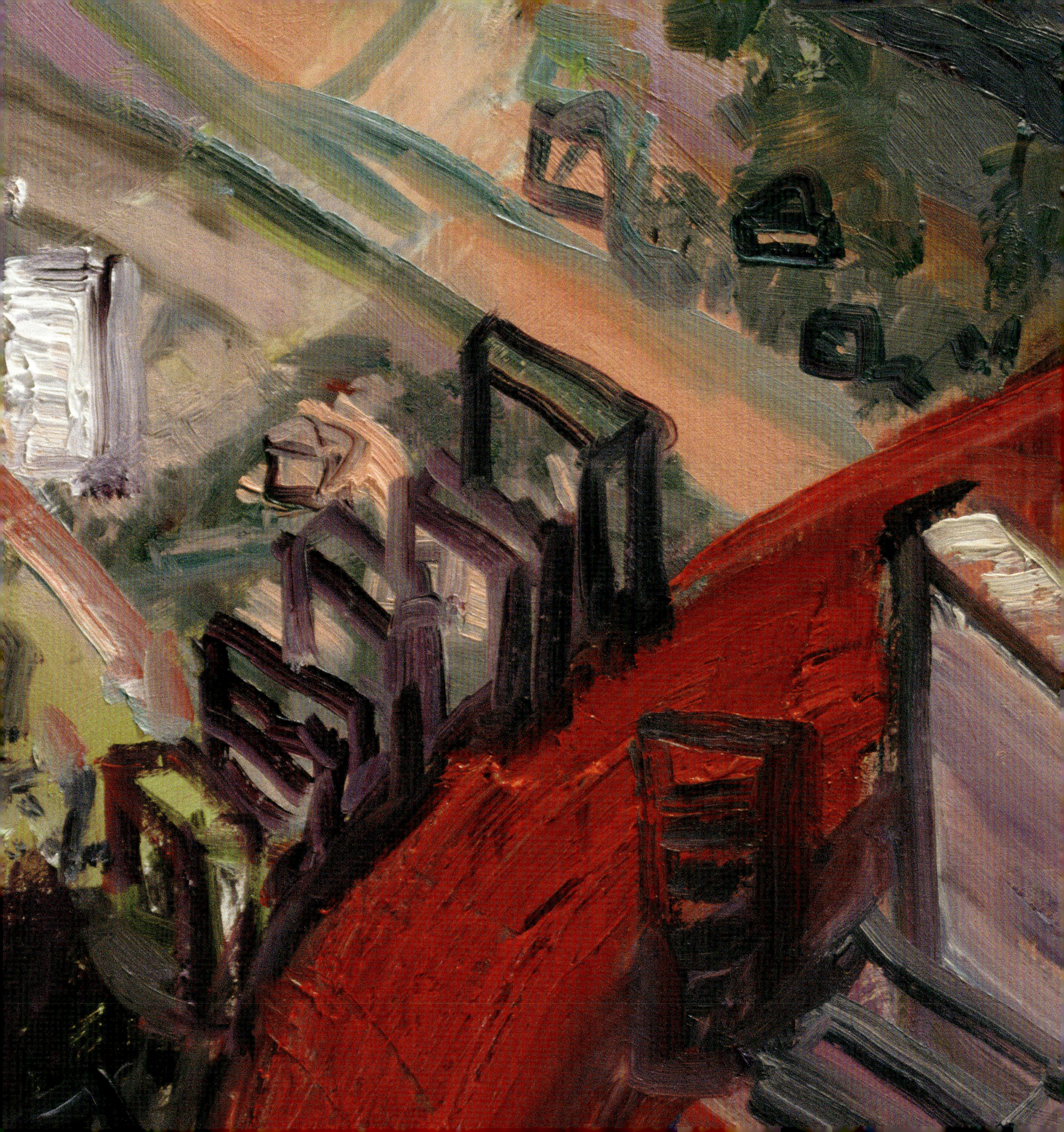

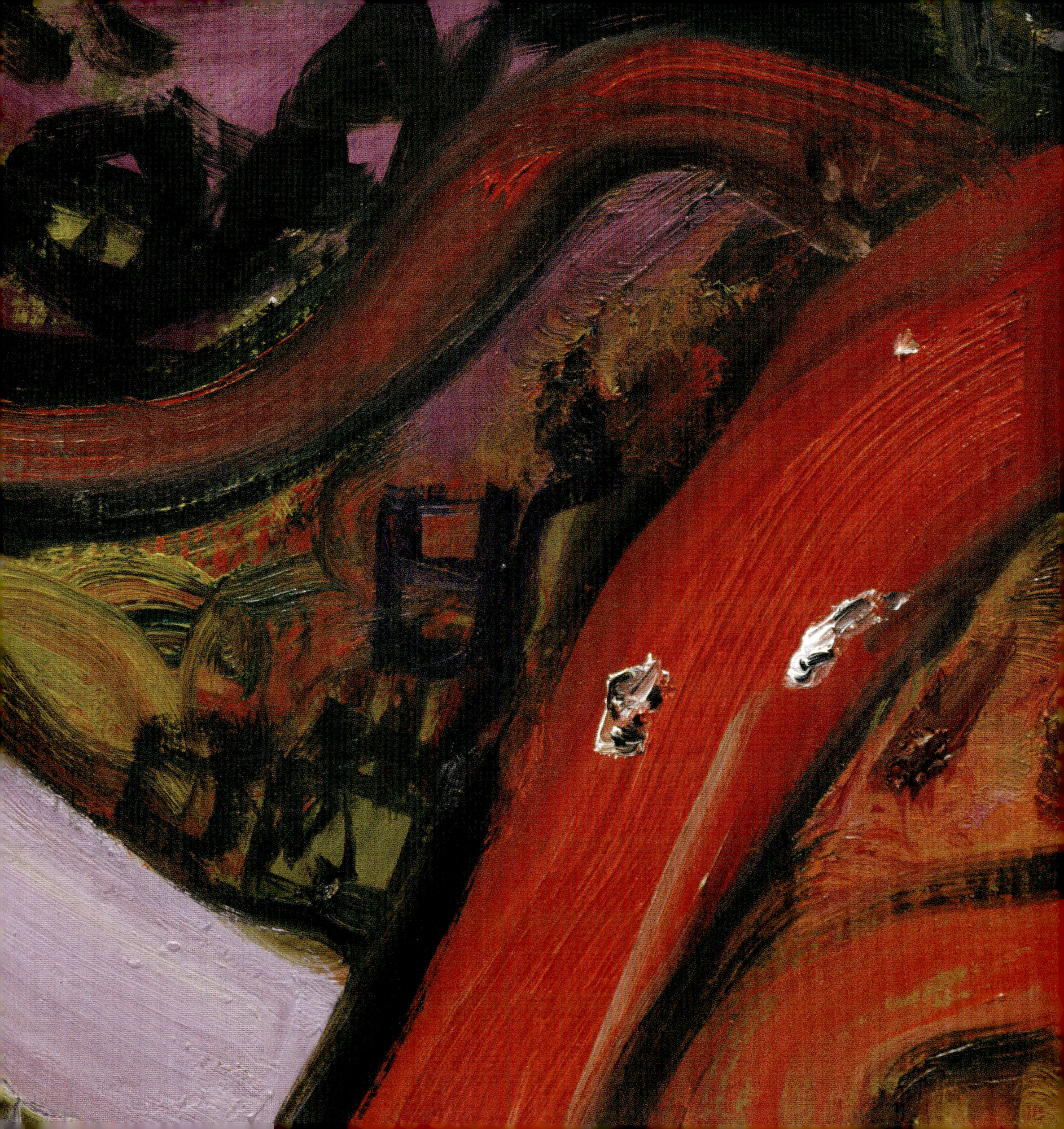

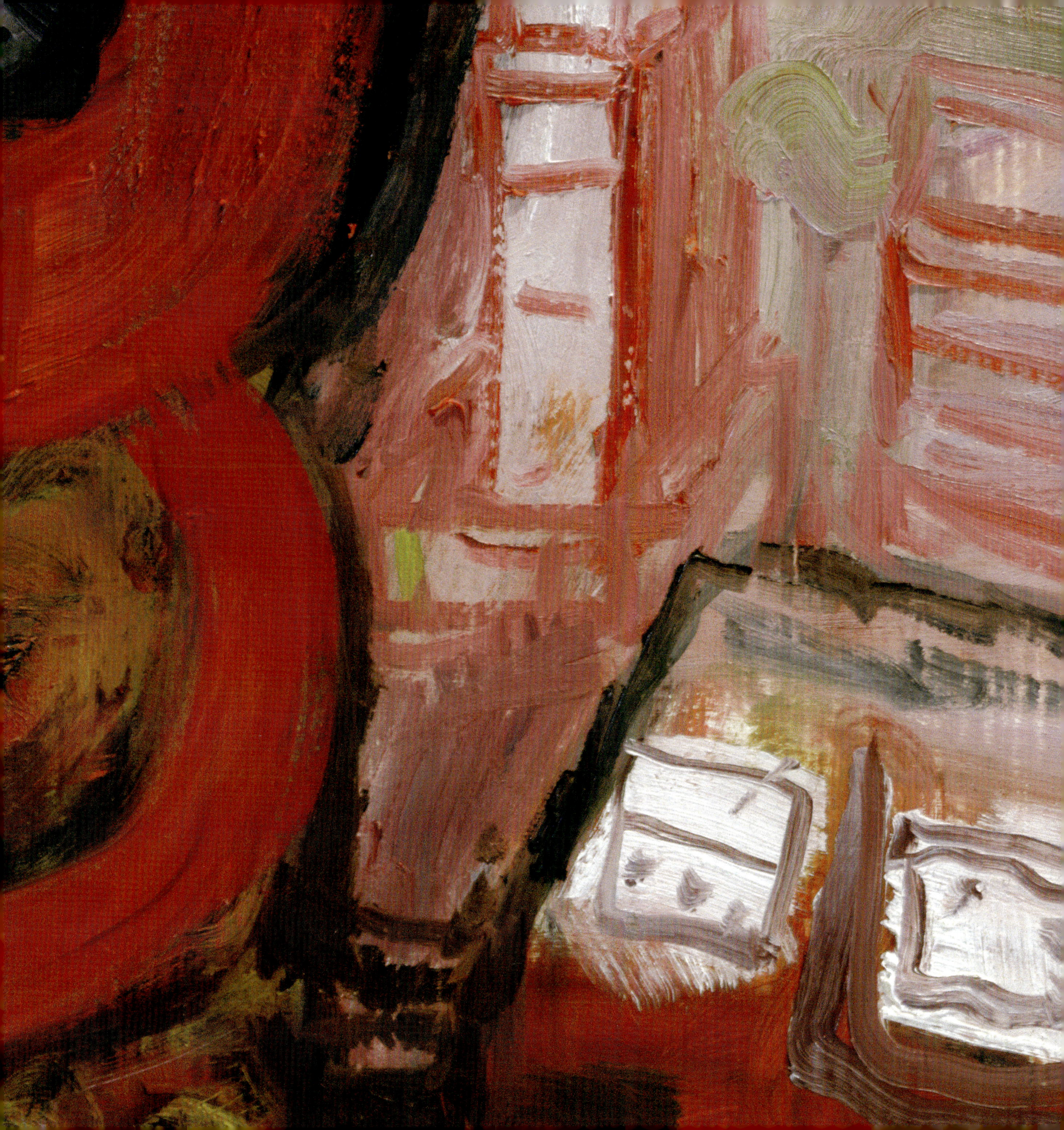

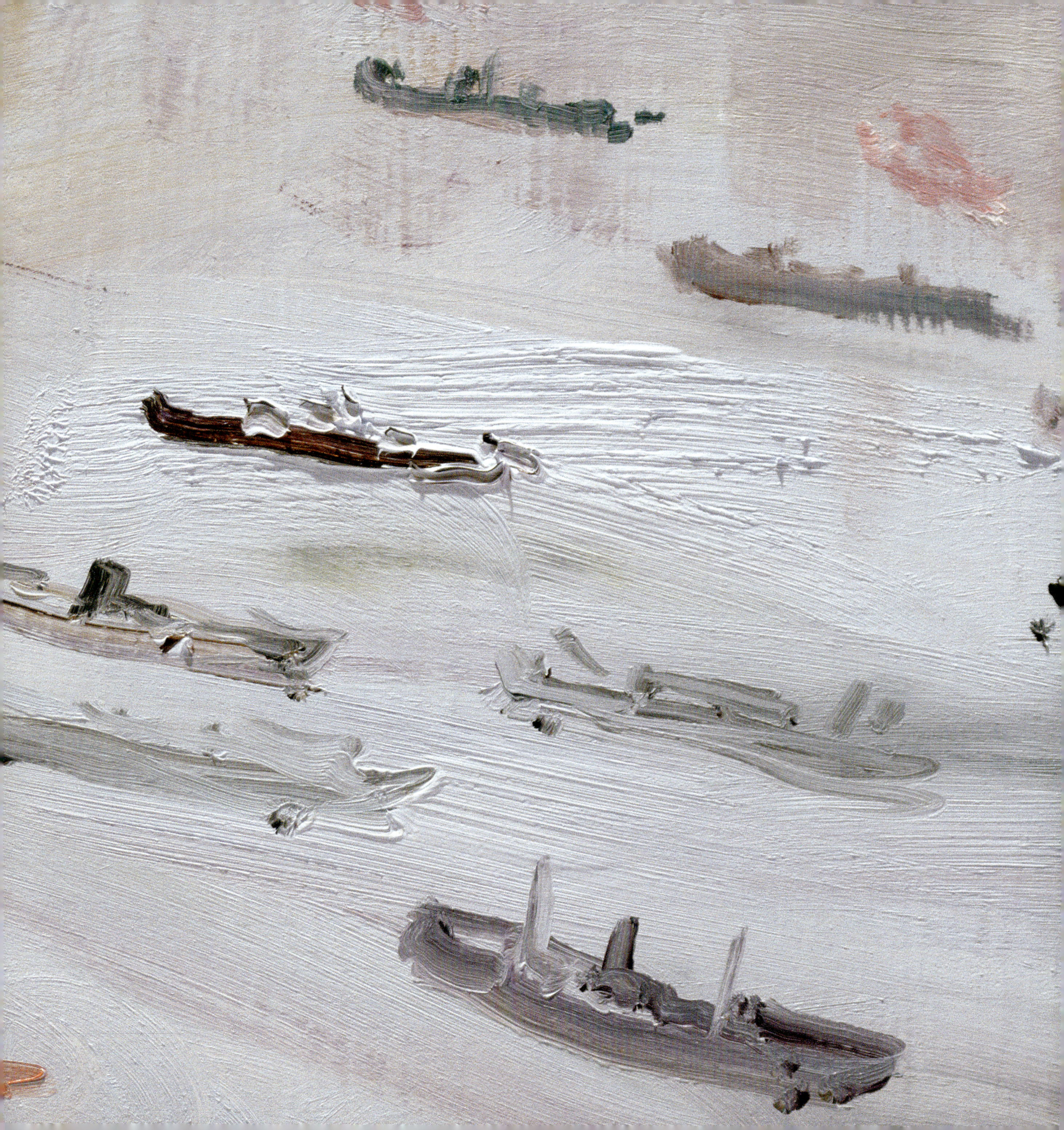

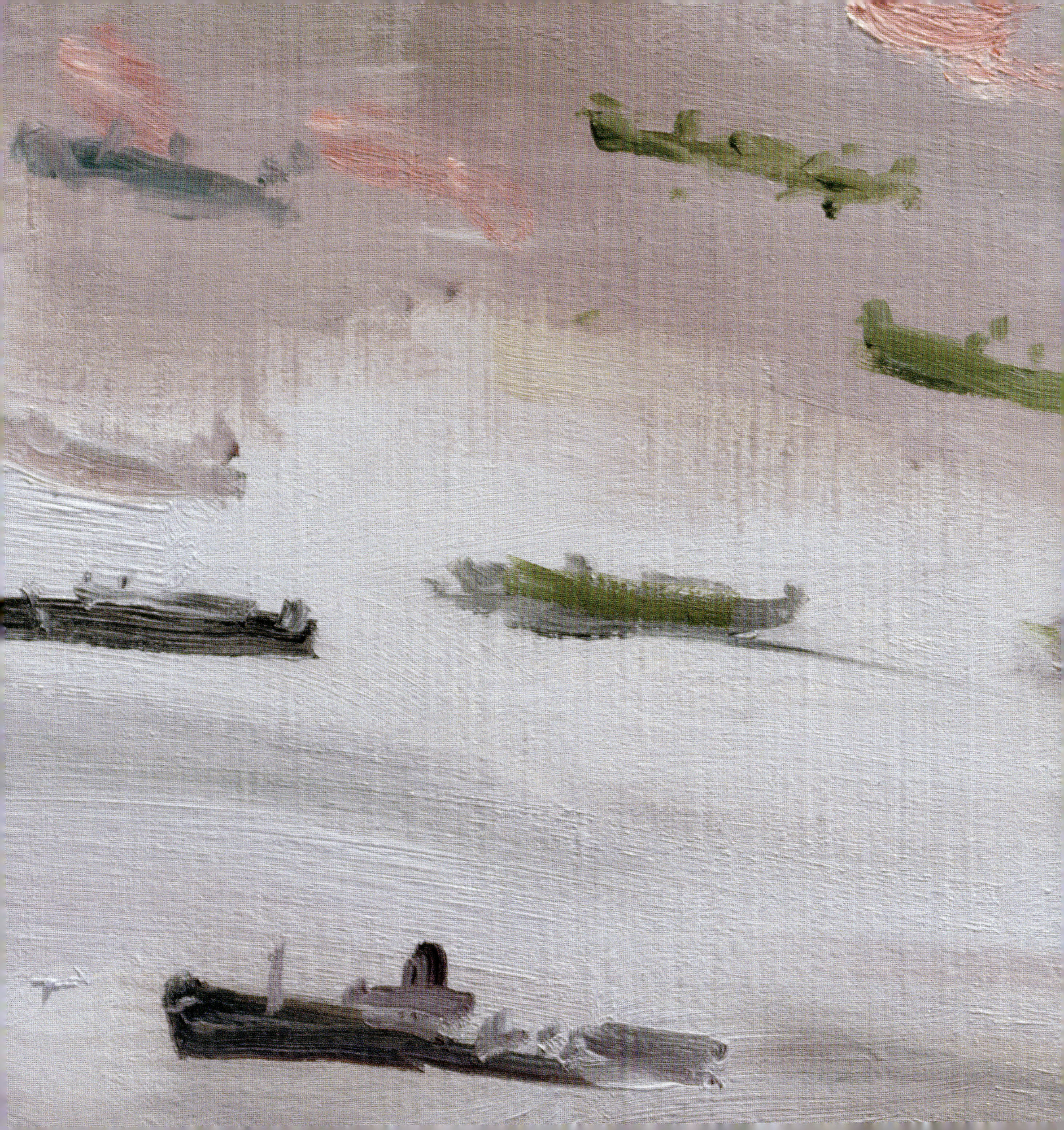

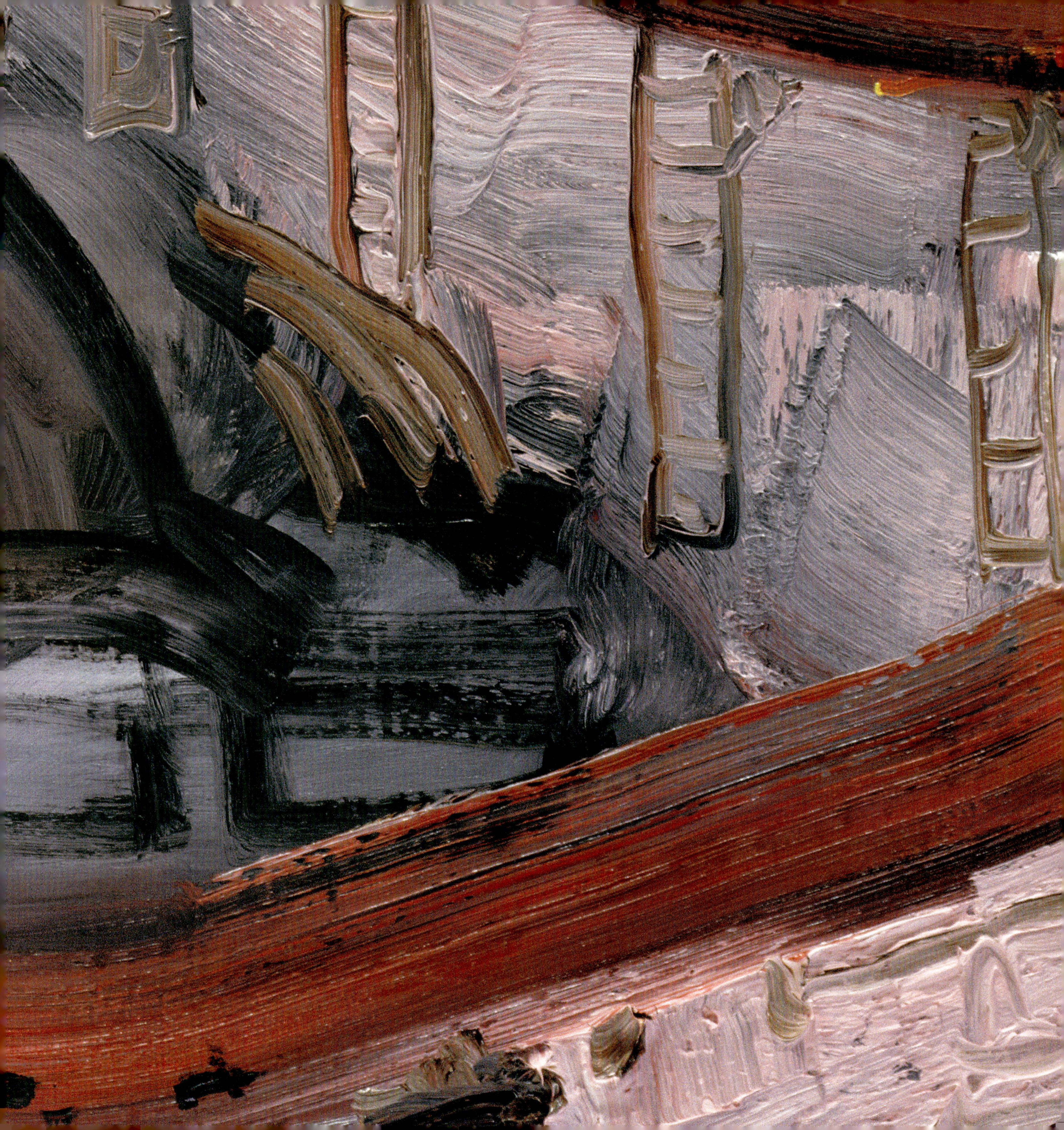

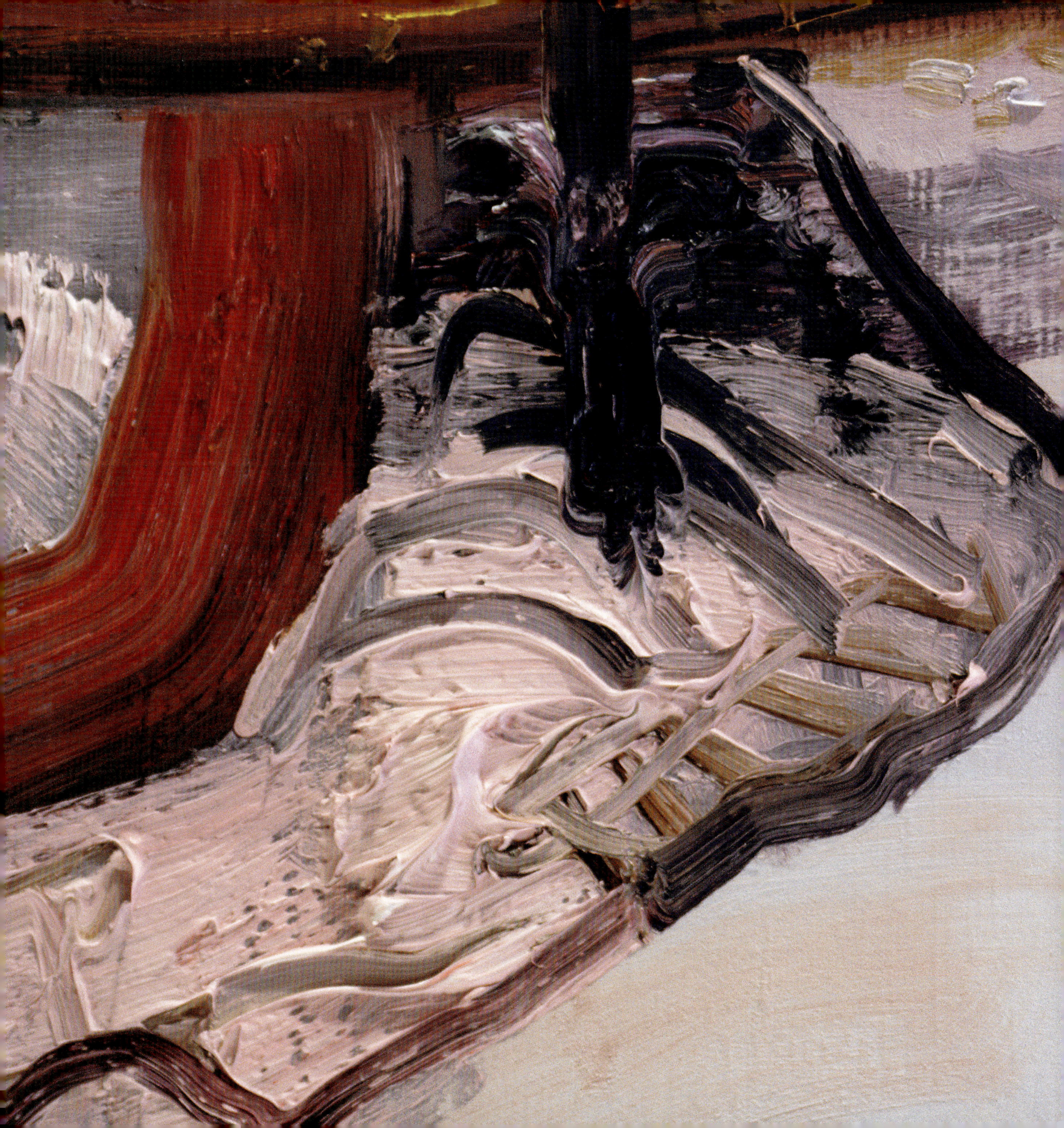

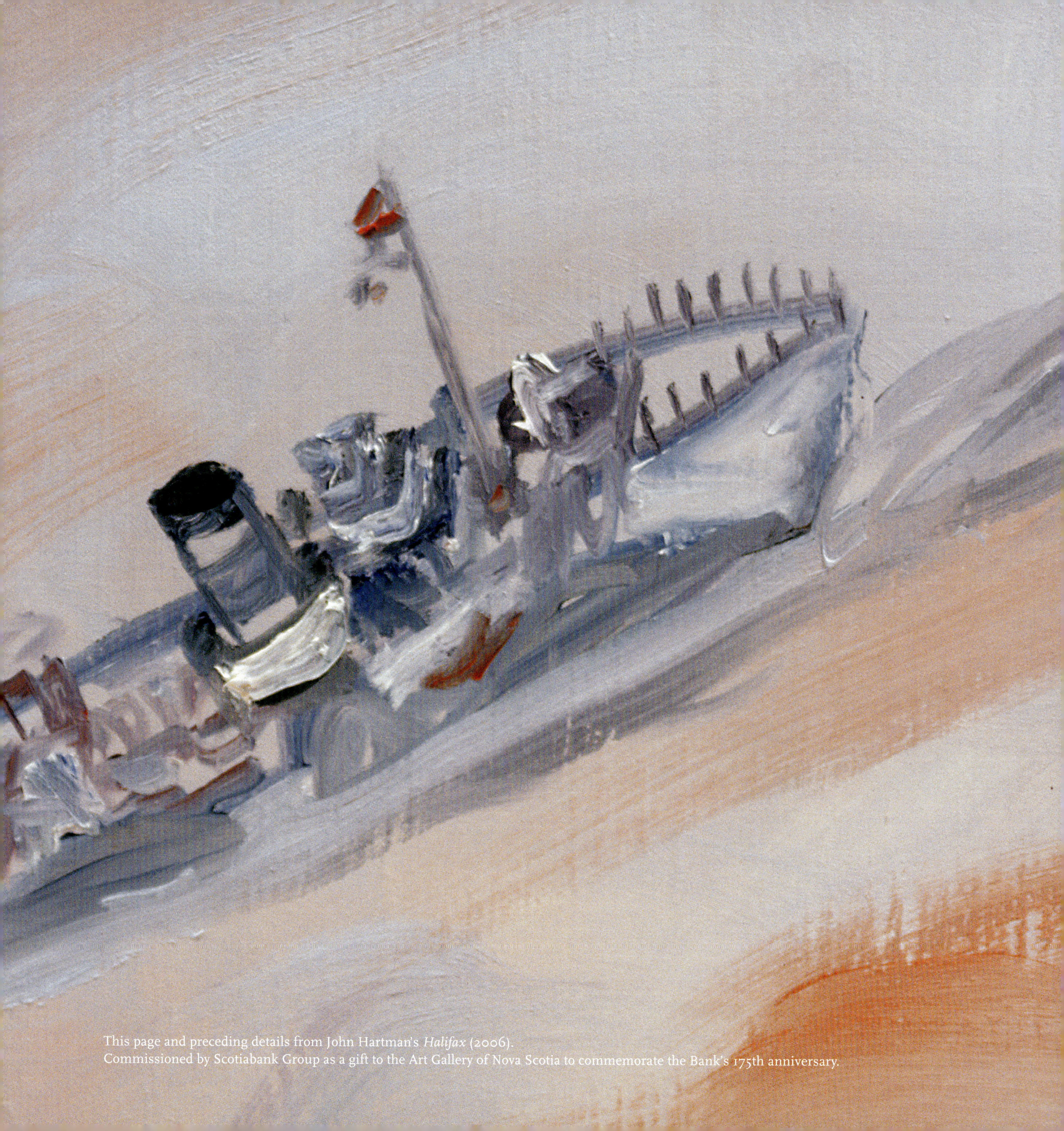

This page and preceding details from John Hartman's *Halifax* (2006).
Commissioned by Scotiabank Group as a gift to the Art Gallery of Nova Scotia to commemorate the Bank's 175th anniversary.

CITIES JOHN HARTMAN

CALGARY

GLASGOW

HALIFAX

HAMILTON

LONDON

MONTREAL

NEW YORK

OWEN SOUND

PARRY SOUND

PORT SEVERN

ST. JOHN'S

TORONTO

VANCOUVER

JOHN

DENNIS REID
NOAH RICHLER
STUART REID

CITIES

HARTMAN

Scotiabank Group™
175 YEARS

To cross the world as Hartman does—to soar over the land to its very horizon—is the delirious, beautiful act.

NOAH RICHLER

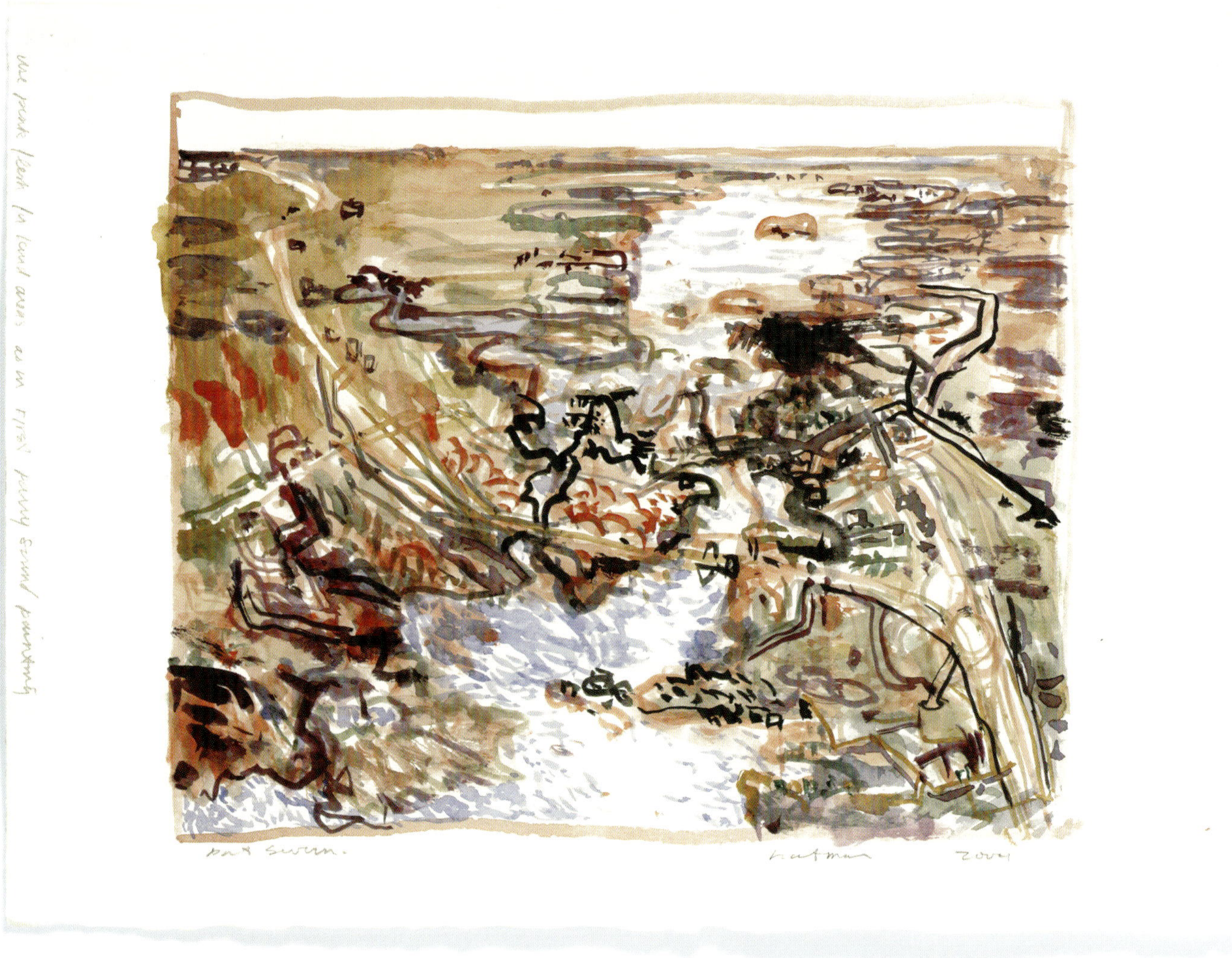

STUDY FOR PORT SEVERN
2004
Watercolour on paper
28.5 x 30 cm (11.25 x 12.75 inches)

PREFACE

DENNIS REID

All artists look closely at the work of other artists. It is one of the ways they learn, how they develop. All too often, however, and particularly when they've engaged with the work of a great master, they succumb to that mastery and lose themselves, as is so evident from the countless "in the manner of" or "from the school of" works that litter the history of art. Then there are those exceptional individuals who engage with another's work in a deeply reflective manner, trying out what they've learned from their looking, testing it, challenging its limits and expanding it in an apparent dialogue with works of art completed decades or centuries ago. So confidently committed are they to their own vision that their conversation with the earlier work easily rises to the prior work's sophistication, embracing its rich resources while subtly turning them to their own specific creative needs. John Hartman is such an artist.

We first met in 1983 when, wanting to present at the Art Gallery of Ontario an exhibition of the long overlooked and underrated contemporary of the Group of Seven, W. J. Wood of Midland, Ontario, I learned that the most knowledgeable person regarding Wood's work, particularly his prints, was a young artist from Midland. He was John Hartman, and we engaged him to work on the exhibition with our Assistant Curator of Historical Canadian Art, Christine Boyanoski. John brought tremendous energy to the project, and long conversations with him about Wood's work opened it up for me in ways that I don't think I could have achieved by myself. John was fascinated with Wood's passionate commitment to a sense of place, to *their* place, the Midland-Penetanguishene region of Georgian Bay, and with how at the same time Wood found ways to connect meaningfully with the larger world. This was reflected both in how the older artist made his art and in how he positioned himself professionally. As I got to know John and his work better over the ensuing months and years, I came to understand the complexity of his relationship to Wood's art and life, how his profound understanding of his admirable antecedent fuelled the realization of his own vision.

I also found increasing pleasure in talking with John about other artists he admired, especially, in recent years, David Milne, who spent six critical years of his life near where the Severn River empties into the eastern end of Georgian Bay. During his time there (1933 through 1939), Milne effectively transformed his vision, and I was delighted to discover that John shares with me a high appreciation of this later period of the great Canadian painter's work. It was thrilling to see him engage enthusiastically in his own painting with issues raised by Milne's, and then to see this discourse turned so effectively to John's own vision. It's important to stress, however, that his art is not "about" the art of others. This might loom somewhat larger for me than for other viewers only because of the privilege of our conversations. John Hartman's art is thoroughly rooted in its own reality. The place depicted is vitally present in every painting, but no more so than the artist's hand and mind.

DENNIS REID is Director of Collections and Research and Senior Curator of Canadian Art at the Art Gallery of Ontario, Toronto.

SPONSOR'S FOREWORD

SCOTIABANK GROUP

CITIES: JOHN HARTMAN is the fine art component of Scotiabank's 175th anniversary, and a focal point of our celebrations in cities across Canada, as well as in cities around the world.

Scotiabank is pleased to be the Presenting Sponsor of *Cities: John Hartman*. This multi-faceted sponsorship includes this book, a touring exhibition, and the painting *Halifax* (2006)—illustrated on the cover and pages 52–53 of this book—commissioned as our gift to the Art Gallery of Nova Scotia to commemorate our 175th anniversary and 175 years of history in that city.

John Hartman is one of Canada's most important artists, and is at the height of his impressive career. His paintings provide us with a relevant and fresh point of view on the cities he is exploring, including Toronto, Halifax, Vancouver, and Montreal, and—appropriately for Scotiabank, which is Canada's most international bank—London and New York.

As with his *Big North: The Paintings of John Hartman*, which we were proud to sponsor from 1999 to 2001, this exhibition will give audiences the opportunity to enjoy an aesthetic experience that stays with them long after leaving the gallery. We know that our clients and the viewing public will appreciate the dynamic images presented here, which capture the spirit of cities, and are at once full of energy and thought-provoking.

The Scotiabank Group of Companies shares a long and rich history with the communities featured in *Cities: John Hartman*, and we are proud of our leadership role in preserving Canada's arts, culture, and heritage, from our donations and sponsorships such as this one to our own notable Corporate Archives and Fine Art Collection. We are confident that the arts, culture, and heritage sector will benefit from the kind of forward-looking partnership between the private sector and public galleries that is exemplified by *Cities: John Hartman*.

This special publication, a Canadian product by an all-Canadian project team, will serve as a record of this landmark exhibition, as well as a touchstone of Scotiabank's strong belief in Canadian arts, culture, and heritage.

Rick Waugh

RICK WAUGH, PRESIDENT AND CEO, SCOTIABANK GROUP

Scotiabank Group™ 175 YEARS

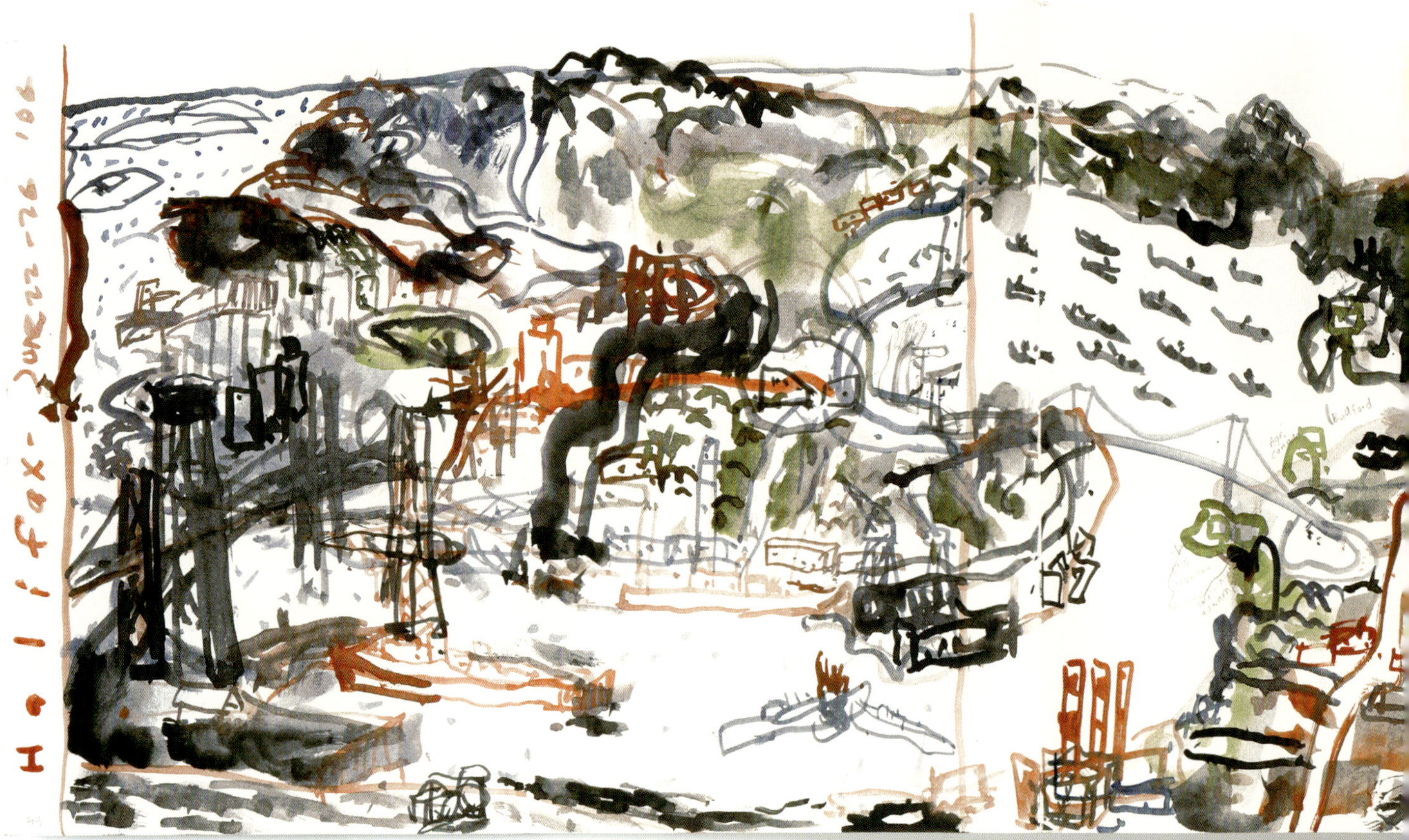

HALIFAX FROM DARTMOUTH
2006
Watercolour and graphite on paper; Concertina folding sketchbook 1, pp. 44–47, bound paper, 138 pages
24 x 17 cm (9.5 x 6.5 inches), folded

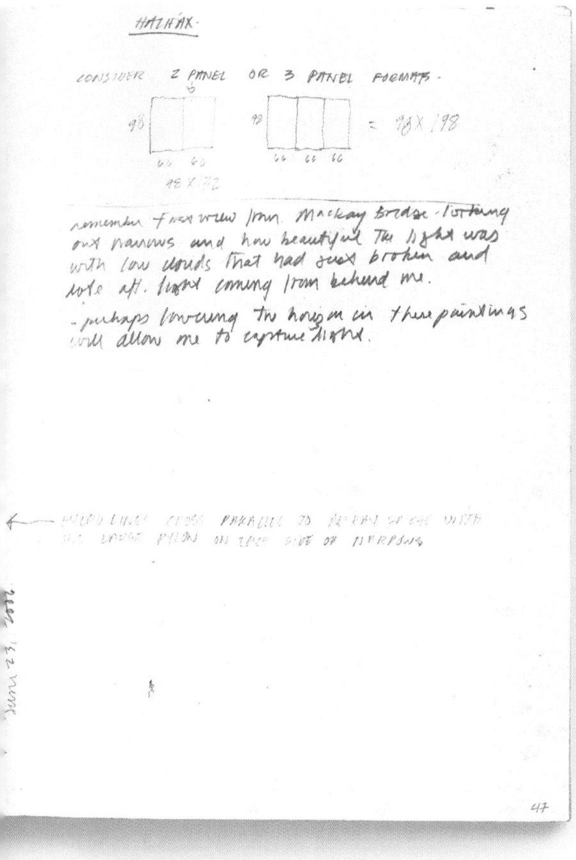
HALIFAX.
CONSIDER 2 PANEL OR 3 PANEL FORMATS.
perhaps lowering the horizon in these paintings will allow me to capture light.

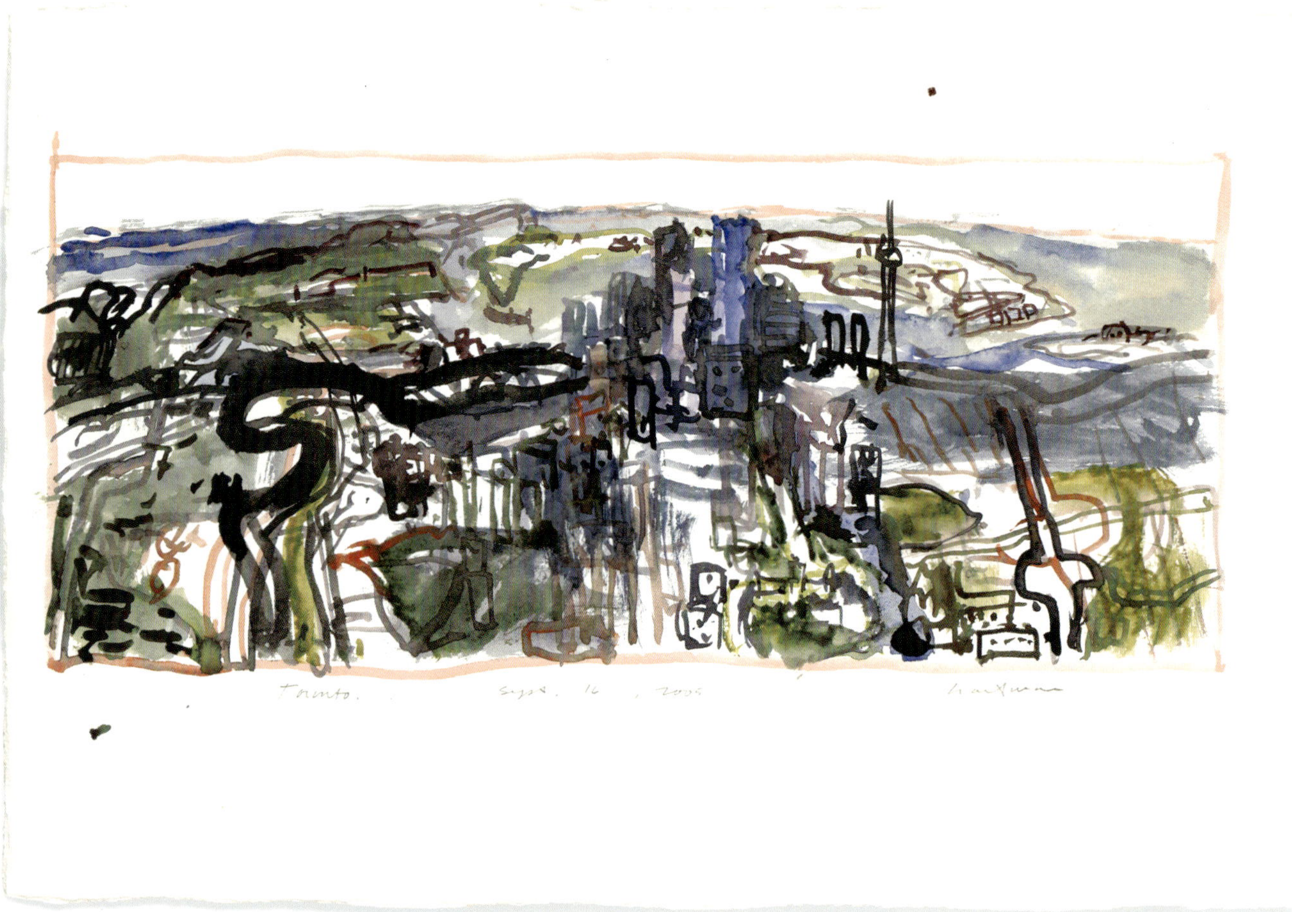

TORONTO
2005
Watercolour on paper
27 x 39 cm (10.5 x 15.25 inches)

ICARUS NEED NOT HAVE DIED

NOAH RICHLER

SOUTHERN ONTARIO, MAY 2006. The skyscrapers of Toronto are built on glacial debris deposited east of the Niagara Escarpment some two million years ago, over a bed of lime shale that was laid another four hundred and fifty million years before, during the Paleozoic era. It is the end of day, the rush hour. In my rear-view mirror, the tall buildings of the city appear like giants looking down from a great height, huddled together on the receding plateau as if leery of just what action the busy streets around their feet might bring. The city is a delta, and these highways are rivers depositing a new millennium's debris at the foot of the old escarpment. Buildings, cars, people. By Lake Ontario, the sediment gathers.

Above the streaming lines of traffic the sky is dark—grey and brooding, dire black in parts. Magnesium-white streaks of lightning cross the sky in jagged horizontal lines. They do not touch the ground, these shocks of electricity that remind the complacent of just how menacing nature can be. The sky is a register of memory, its dramatic display of lightning an indication of our small and fleeting presence upon the larger territory—and of our believing that we are separate from nature because the materials that we use are "man-made." We assume, in our effrontery, that nature can be contained. Because we do not see the whole, we forget that we are a part of the land and that we too are subject to its fundamental physical laws.

Further up the tarmac river, the human settlement diminishes. Around Barrie, a town already larger than most of the cities of the Canadian nineteenth century were, industrial parks become malls and the malls become houses and the houses open fields—green and brimming and ready to explode, nature as it is in Canada, impatient for the end of winter and the short, urgent opportunity of the truncated northern summer. The route to John Hartman's Lafontaine studio takes me through Elmvale and Wyevale and then Perkinsfield, where the long Franco-Ontarian pedigree of Simcoe County—land that was once Huron and then a spiritual battleground for Jesuit missionaries harvesting reluctant souls—announces its history in the sudden appearance of French signage over stores and playing fields. This prior incarnation of the land was one of the first preoccupations of the artist I was travelling to see, the Aboriginal and French stories as much in the vault of his world as the day's spent lightning was in mine. In Hartman's *Wendake* cycle of

… as I stepped out of the cocoon of the car that had brought me, the rhythms of the country seemed strange and untoward, like the calm of a civilization that had flourished prior to the twenty-first-century urban storm.

paintings, the parts the Jesuits and the Huron played in the settling of this part of Ontario are implied through icons that the artist appears to have sketched impulsively into the big skies that have always been a feature of his work. But they are deliberate. They are acknowledgements of *presences*—for history, in Canada, is written on the territory; it is in the air. It is spoken on reserves and in Franco-Ontarian hamlets such as Lafontaine—where Hartman lives and keeps his studio—and Penetanguishene, the Franco-Ontarian community outside the waterside industrial town of Midland, where Hartman grew up. The "lakers"—the freighters that used to travel over Lake Huron from Port Arthur, now Thunder Bay—used to be built here. They would carry their cargo of grain to Midland, where it would be put on the trains east to Montreal. Today, the docks where the lakers were once lined up side by side in their winter berths are idle. The elevators where the grain was stored are empty. The mills that were busy until the white pine was all felled are still. Midland now provides scenes for photographers wishing to remember a more gregarious industrial age by recording its absences and implores writers and painters to resurrect these spaces with their stories. Midland is a quiet place, and the cottagers who boost the region's economy come to these parts to get away—they travel, as I had done, *against* the forceful urban tide.

Past Lafontaine and towards the lake, the fields surrounding the Hartman place were empty and quiet. I'd come to see Hartman begin a painting of Vancouver, the next of his urban landscapes as seen from on high—New York, London, Glasgow, Montreal, Toronto, and Calgary were the other cities that Hartman had painted for the evolving series—and as I stepped out of the cocoon of the car that had brought me, the rhythms of the country seemed strange and untoward, like the calm of a civilization that had flourished prior to the twenty-first-century urban storm. Arriving in the pleasant countryside, I found myself wondering to what extent the paintings of John Hartman were the result of the trips he'd made against the inexorable flow into Toronto—of having no choice but to acknowledge the city's furious engine.

HARTMAN, IN HIS EARLY FIFTIES NOW, is a lean, silver-haired, good-looking man with a habit of peering at you above the light wire spectacles that sit at the end of his nose. He welcomed me, and led me past the old farmhouse and the vegetable garden, where his wife, Trish, was culling asparagus, into the studio at the foot of the drive. "Cities drive the modern economy," he said, "not the rural areas that depend on their surplus." He was smiling benignly. It was an obvious thought, not a troubling one, and the impulse behind his "Cities" series of paintings, which was ever growing in scope. For a time the Hartmans lived in Collins, a Native Canadian community on the CN rail line west of Armstrong and north of Thunder Bay. It was during this period, between 1976 and 1981, that Hartman learned to conceive of cities not as "man-made" anomalies but as landscapes that were, in their essence and in their variety of elements, as natural as rocks, rivers, and lakes.

"When I lived in Collins," said Hartman, "I had to come to terms with being the white guy, and one of the things that astonished me about that was realizing the way in which my Western civilization had always tended to regard itself as *separate* from the land, when it would have been much healthier to have conceived of the world as Aboriginals do—as a huge and constantly changing organism—and to regard ourselves as *part* of it. The idea that we are somehow distinct from nature is just a bizarre construct that Western civilization has created."

"Then do you see your work as political?" I asked.

"No," said Hartman. "I'm interested in how the erection of cities has altered the sites they're built on, but I'm not actually attaching any *moral* value to these phenomena. I'm not saying that cities are bad because we pollute the harbours, for instance, but that we have to realize that what we do will affect landscapes by virtue of our using these sites. I really do see us as *part* of the landscape, and cities as examples of an extraordinary overlay of human activity."

A great triptych of Vancouver was drying on the northern wall and, as I contemplated it, Hartman said, "You know, people might look at what I paint and say that I'm making a statement about how cities pollute the water, or something like that, but I'm not. Above all, I'm trying to make a piece of art, and it could be that I just like the colour red. Most of all, what I am working with and responding to is colour."

In the middle of the studio, on a flat that could be moved to catch the best light, a large blank canvas, 78 by 90 inches, was waiting for the painting of Burrard Inlet that Hartman was about to begin. Some of his sketches and works on paper were stored in metal cartographer's cabinets behind it, and other finished paintings were drying or neatly stacked. A painting in which lilies were the central feature honoured Hartman's recently deceased mother. (The lilies had belonged

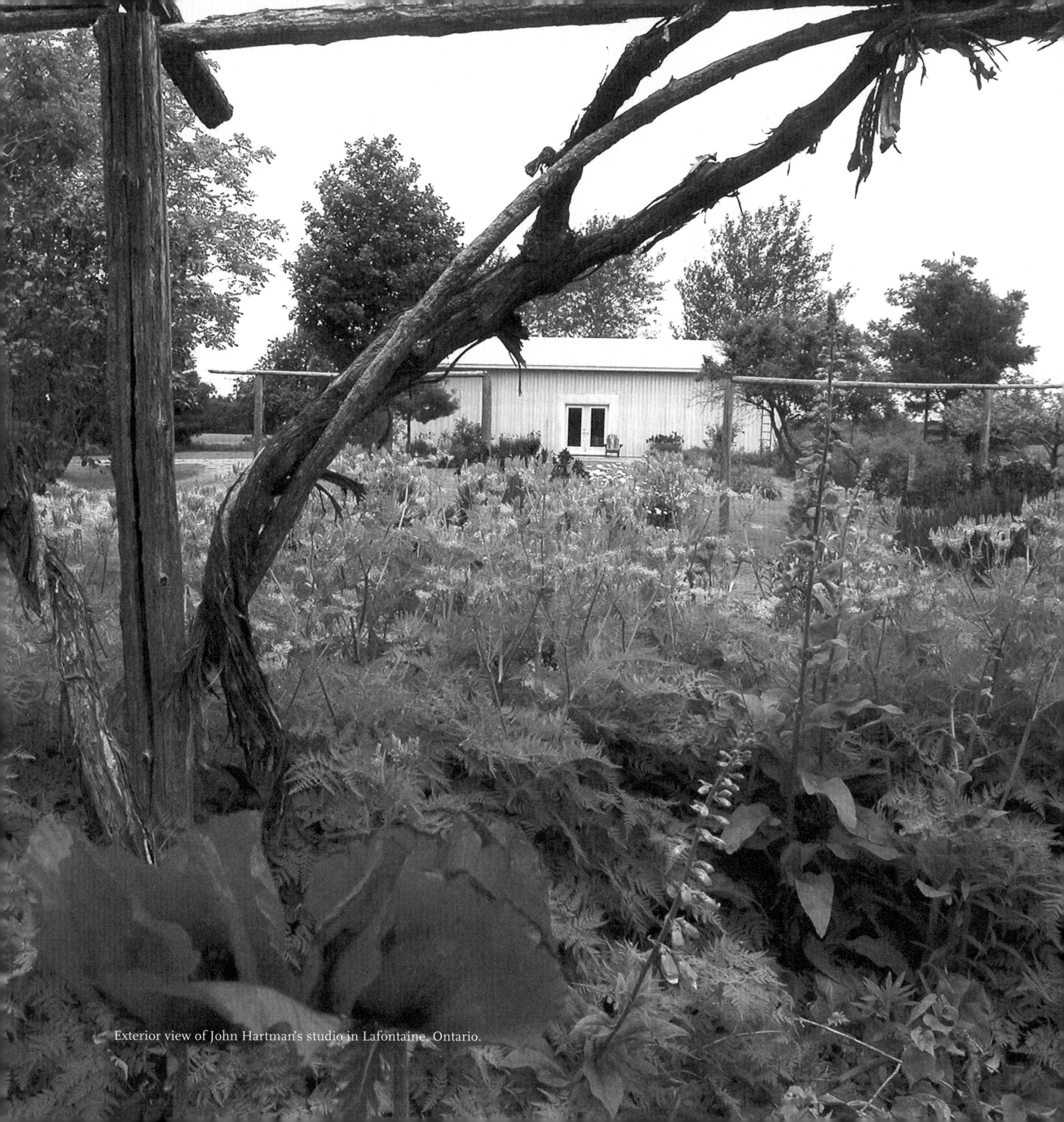

Exterior view of John Hartman's studio in Lafontaine, Ontario.

to a bouquet from her funeral.) Against a set of racks containing various finished works stood a large painting of Toronto. The painting was unresolved. It demanded either more work—or, as happens only on rare occasions, to be burned.

"That's half of a diptych that I've been working on for three months now—and that's really unusual," said Hartman, following my gaze. "It's a problem of composition, I think. I don't know that I had a big enough idea to start with."

"Is there some fundamental decision that you need to make about each city painting before you start?"

"Yes," said Hartman. "There always has to be one essential characteristic about a city or where it is that I can paint towards. With Manhattan, it had to do with the remarkable density of the buildings. In Halifax, it has to do with the incredible site that the city sits on, and all the unusual and interesting stuff that happens around its edges—the power plants and docks and refineries and places for decommissioning ships and all that. With Vancouver, it was the physical layout of the place—its sheer beauty and the way the container ships come in from and out to the sea, or how, in that area at the base of False Creek, you have a knotted configuration of railway lines and highways, so that immediately I know that the challenge of the painting will be to find the right balance between the land and the sea."

Typically, Hartman's research involves surveying the city he plans to paint from a small plane, taking aerial photographs, and, on the ground, recording his impressions in watercolour in the concertina sketchbooks that he favours. Hartman also collects postcards and photographs from books, any view that might prove useful. In the studio, he keeps a computer close at hand in order to easily reference his collection of digital photographs. The notebooks and other printed materials are also nearby. He uses an old knee-high wooden washstand, once his grandfather's, to store his paints, his rags, and the glass pane on which he mixes his paints. The washstand is layered with drips and wipes but is actually rather neat. He is a man with a method.

Hartman dips his brush in Indian Red, the russet oil paint he uses to lay the idea of a work before he begins, and starts by making small central marks at the top and bottom of the canvas. Next, he applies a first stroke from left to right—where, soon enough, ocean (the Pacific) will meet sky. The adventure has begun. As in Hartman's earlier paintings of Newfoundland and Georgian Bay, the line of the horizon bends, as if delineating the very curvature of the Earth. The bend appears casual, but is one of the ways in which the painter shows that our phenomenological perception of the world is altered by the effect of the stories that allow us to remember it. No one is actually able to discern with the naked eye that the Earth is round—we can only calculate as much—but the story is a part of our knowledge and so we accept Hartman's curved line. There is always this

There is always this play, in Hartman's work, between "true" information about a place and the stories that animate it—for when we stand before a Hartman painting we are entering not into a literal landscape, but into the painter's vision.

play, in Hartman's work, between "true" information about a place and the stories that animate it—for when we stand before a Hartman painting we are entering not into a literal landscape, but into the painter's vision. Of the bloody history of Jesuit martyrdom and first contact that he strove to capture in several of the *Wendake* paintings, including *Brébeuf and Lalemant* (1993), Hartman wrote, "When I am in Midland Harbour I am aware of this history, of my own memories and of the objects I see in front of me. For me, the landscape is all of these because it is something I construct in my mind. As I paint it, its reality becomes greater."

In his "Cities" series, Hartman is still working from the middle space—that space between the world as it is and as it ends up being represented in his art—but he is doing so in the other direction. This time, as he paints it, its reality becomes *less*.

"I really love what digital photography can do," says Hartman, who has opened a binder of aerial photographs and set it upon a footstool by the painting. "With a sketch you tend to focus in and eliminate what's around you, and the simulacrum of the digital photograph really puts you in the spot. The thing about digital photography is that I can make it see the way I see when I sketch, by zooming in upon a detail."

"It's interesting to me," I said, "that you are able to use digital photography to such advantage. David Hockney argued that technological advances in the Old Masters' ability to refract images at the end of the sixteenth century accounted for quantum leaps in their ability to paint from life.[1] Is that something you believe?"

"Hockney's critics were right in that he'd probably pushed the point too far," said Hartman, "as painters only needed to see an image in the box of a camera obscura in order to be able to sketch and paint it, rather than needing to project and trace it. The real advance on the Middle Ages was

[1] See David Hockney, *Secret Knowledge: Rediscovering the Lost Techniques of the Old Masters* (New York: Viking Studio, 2001).

that painters learned to see the world from a single viewpoint. I can understand how in the fifteenth and sixteenth centuries, when so many were keen on establishing rational ideas in nature, it would have been appealing to be able to impose that sort of order on things. The possibility of a single viewpoint would have been revolutionary. But now it's as if we've reached the end of that road, so that a lot of twentieth- and early twentieth-first-century painting has been about getting *away* from a single viewpoint. Certainly, my paintings have always had many."

Hartman pointed to an area at the bottom of the canvas that was swiftly becoming the south side of Burrard Inlet.

"For instance, this bit here is taken fairly exactly from the photograph I took while flying overhead, but at the same time the effect is of looking obliquely down at it from a distance, as I did when I was sketching it. Hopefully that gives the painting some motion, rather than it being just an assembly of several static viewpoints."

"I see that you tend to finish one part of the painting and then move on," I said.

"I need to work while the paint is still wet," said Hartman.

The Pacific's blue water had descended past the North Shore and into Burrard Inlet, and swiftly the industrial docks around the inlet and downtown Vancouver were beginning to take shape. Office buildings were burgeoning and train tracks and highways claiming their place and thrusting towards the city.

"At this point the painting is still a drawing, because I haven't yet resolved any of the questions of colour that are constantly running through my mind," said Hartman. "Most painters work from broad effects to more specific, detailed ones, but for me the most dramatic strokes of colour come in last. Do I make the sky light and the water dark? The tonal relationships are still sitting there as a realm of possibilities."

Hartman stepped forward and with a wide brush added great swaths of green, purple, red, and white to the area of Vancouver below False Creek.

"A change of mind?"

"No, but this whole north side of the painting was developed with the same sort of touch and I feel that if I do the same thing over here then it would get monotonous. It's really not very fashionable to talk about beauty these days, but I'm quite happy to concentrate on the *emotional* impact of a place and, frankly, just to make a beautiful painting."

"Are those train tracks or roads?" I asked—still looking, as Hartman's paintings prompt one to do, for a Vancouver I could recognize in the midst of his ecstatic rendition of the place.

"I don't always know," he said.

Hartman was working quickly now, stepping back from the painting from time to time to check the binder or the digital images on his laptop computer. Already the line of coast linking North and then West Vancouver to Horseshoe Bay, and the ridge of snow-capped mountains beyond it, was tied to the city and to the dark promontory of Stanley Park rapidly taking its place in the high centre of the canvas.

"Your work reminds me of battle paintings of the Italian Renaissance," I said, "in which an entire story is told on one canvas. You don't have the legions of soldiers, of course, but your paintings have a similar kind of movement."

"There's a painting in the Alte Pinakothek, in Munich, that Albrecht Altdorfer painted in the early sixteenth century," said Hartman. "It's a panorama of Alexander the Great's defeat of the Persian king Darius III called *The Battle of Issus* (1529) (see p.122, fig. 3). When I was twenty-four I was finally able to visit the Pinakothek, and as I was walking through, I'd seen a number of paintings that did not excite me. But then I turned the corner and there it was—Altdorfer's painting hit me like a lightning bolt, and subsequently I bought a number of reproductions of it and put them in my scrapbooks. It's done from on high: the battle is in the foreground, and in the sky is a banner explaining the action that's taking place. In the distance are cities, mountains, and the sea. There are ships coming into port, and above the sea the sun is setting. I had no idea how I would get there from being a landscape painter, but I knew without question that it was where I wanted to go. The painting keeps your eye moving until you get right to the horizon, where Altdorfer decides to stop and put the sky in. It's as if he is saying that beyond the battle's reach, life goes on."

"Any other influences?"

"Well, Turner, and David Milne, of course. Someone I think of as a great city painter, though his paintings aren't quite as map-like as mine, is Oskar Kokoschka, the Viennese painter of the last century. He'd find a point where he could go up three or four hundred feet and imagine himself higher (see p. 127, fig. 5). A friend of mine once showed me a collection of his oil-painting views in a book and, though I flipped through them very quickly, they must have made a great impression, because even now, thirty or forty years later, I still think of them."

Hartman lined English Bay with a thin stroke of white sand, and the docklands of the inlet with warehouses and piers. The office blocks and condominiums sprouting amid the streets of the downtown core were gaining windows and, to the west, the bridges linking Vancouver with Granville Island and Kitsilano had come into being. BC Place, the city's domed sports stadium, had taken its berth at the bottom of False Creek and had become, curiously, a place where the eye could rest—an oval anomaly amid the squares of buildings, hard lines of docks, and meandering arteries of railroads and highways. At the bottom of the canvas, the water spilling into the harbour had taken on muddy, dirty brown hues. Hartman was adding freighters, some of them moored off English Bay and others on their way to and from the docks. They bobbed in Burrard Inlet like toy boats.

Hartman stepped back from the painting, checked the binder, and shook his head slightly, peering at what he'd done so far over spectacles dropped to the tip of his nose.

"I just left out about a half-mile of shoreline," he said with amusement. "Over here below Lions Gate Bridge and these docks are these great big sulphur piles which are actually"—Hartman moved back towards the canvas and painted a white line over a stretch of industrial docks—"right over *here*."

Hartman perused the painting some more.

"Well, I've certainly committed myself to a bunch of paint, haven't I?"

Occasionally Hartman would scrape paint from an area where the colour or the detail was not quite right (the mountains, Granville Island), and then smear more over it.

"I need the intensity of the right side of the painting to make its way over to the left," he said.

As Hartman applied further touches of paint over areas that were still wet, the colour scheme of the painting was becoming more evident. This version of the West Coast city was all mauves and

Hartman stepped back from the painting, checked the binder, and shook his head slightly, peering at what he'd done so far over spectacles dropped to the tip of his nose.

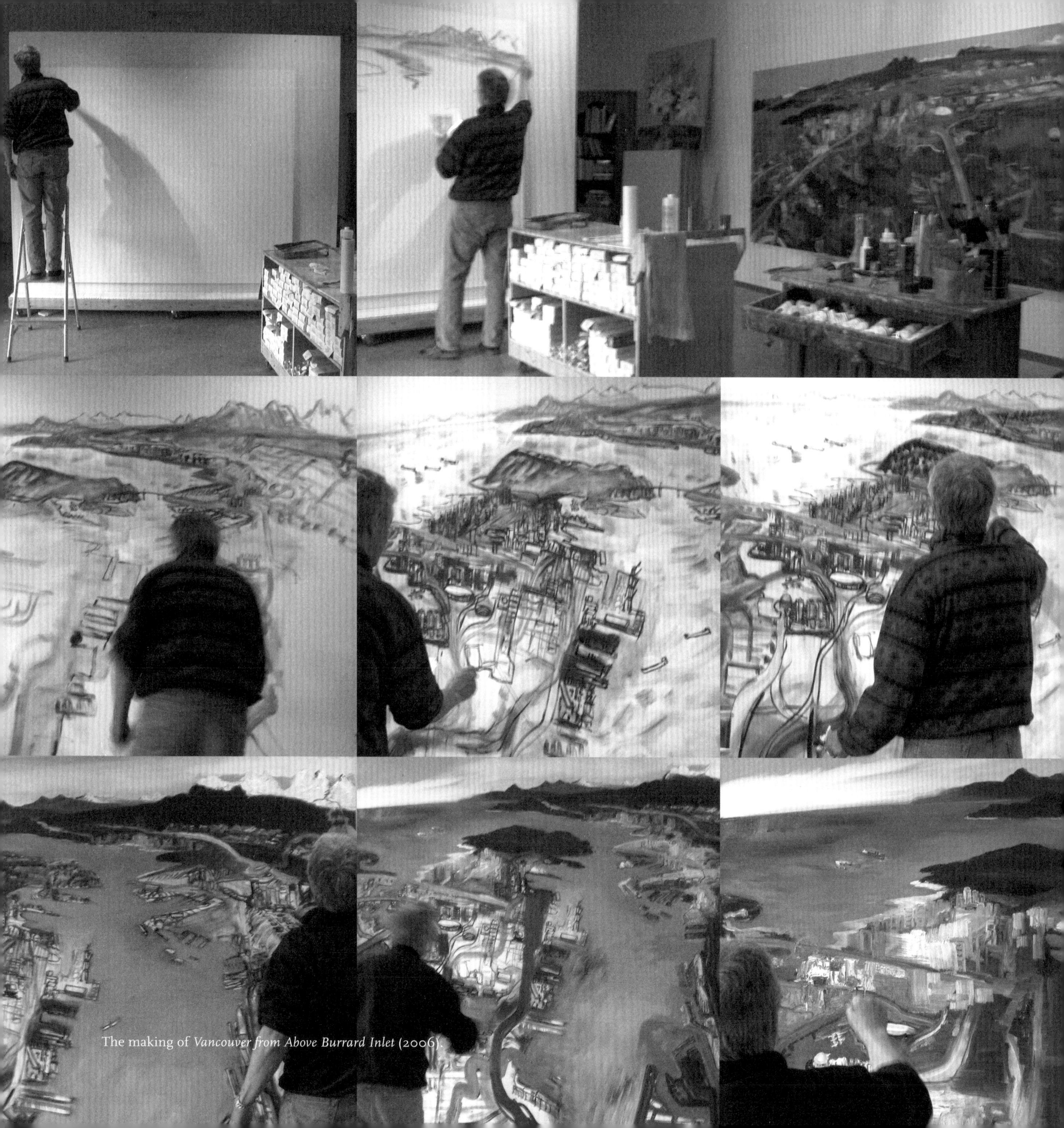

The making of *Vancouver from Above Burrard Inlet* (2006).

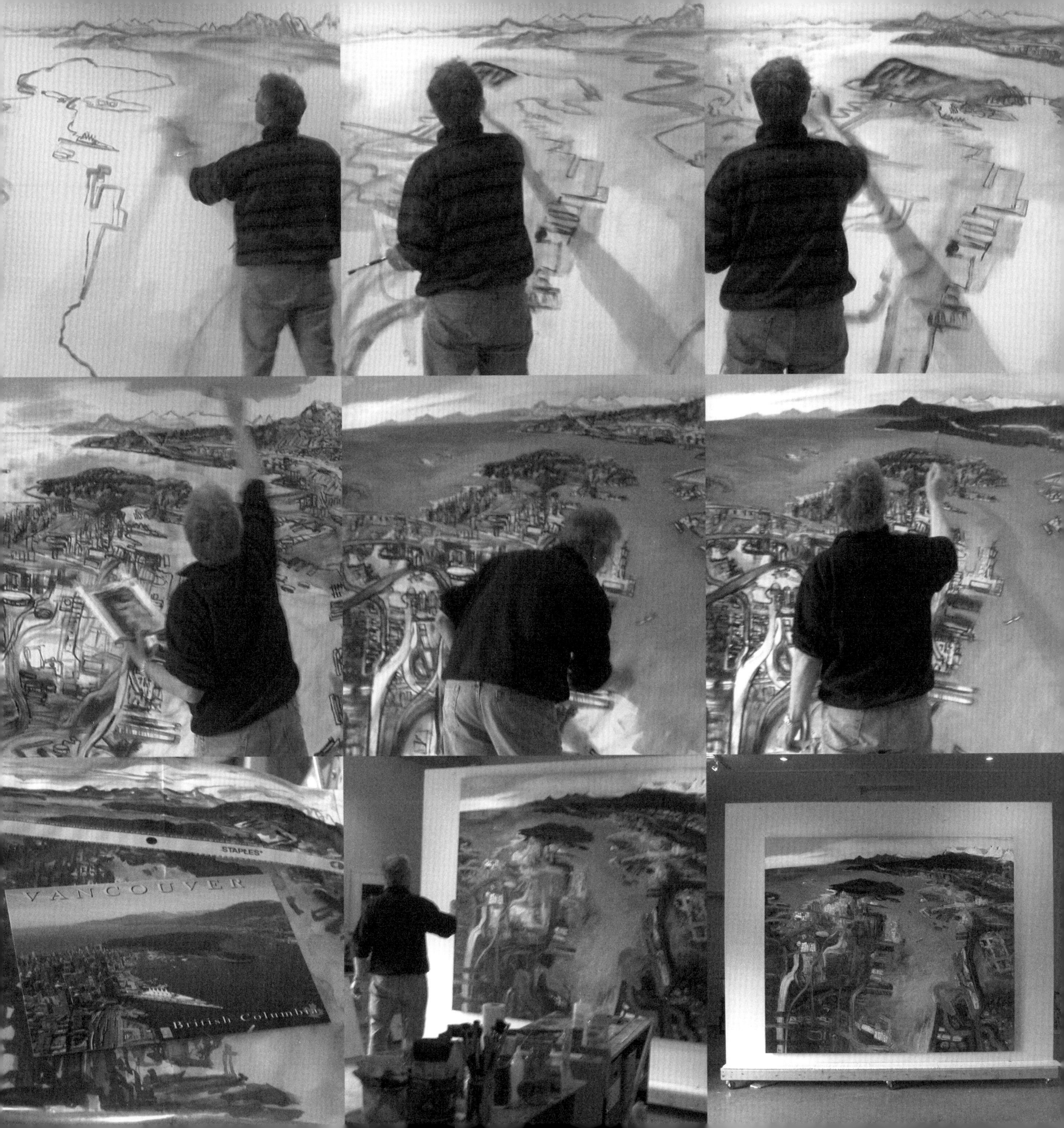
STAPLES
VANCOUVER
British

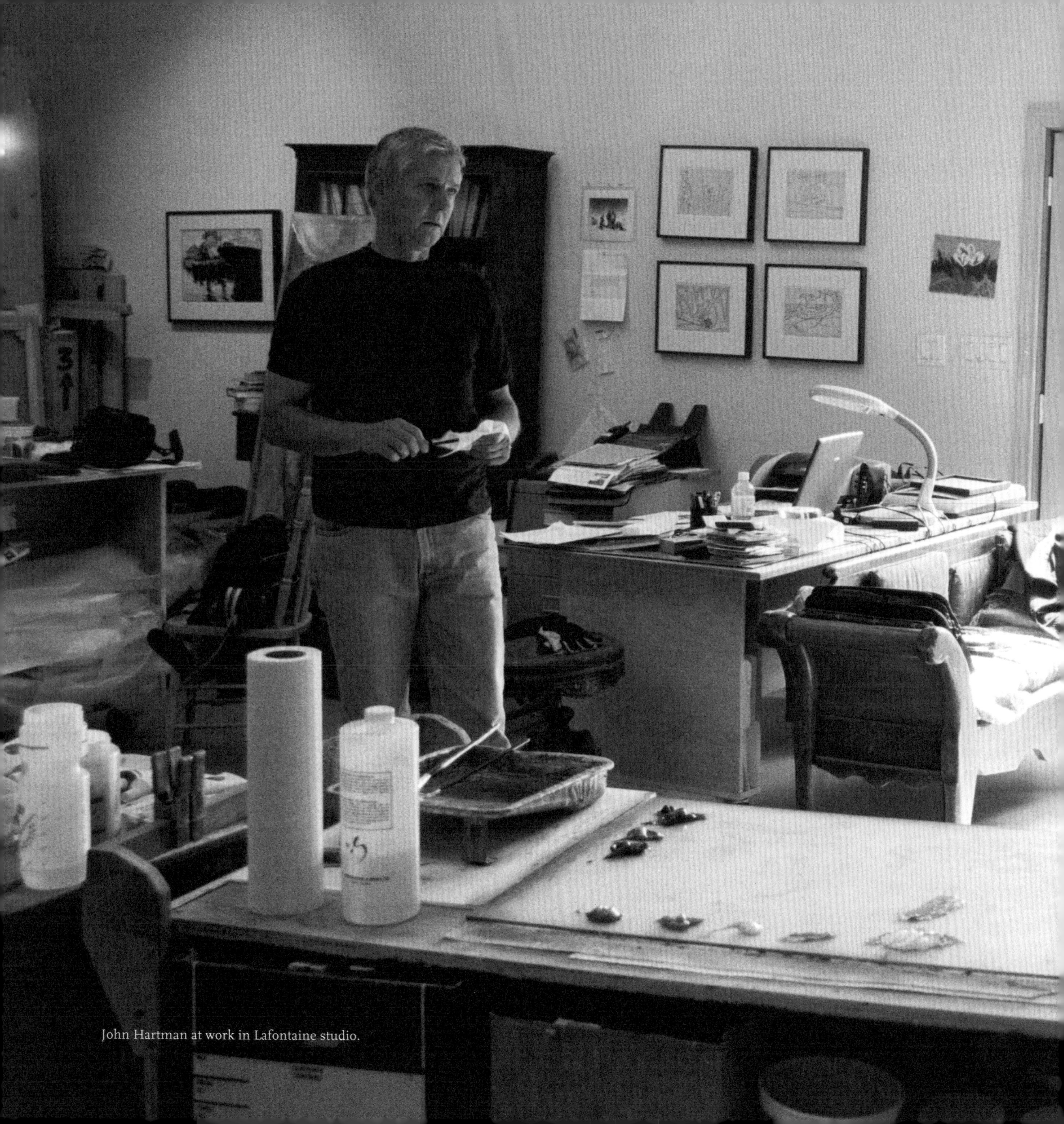

John Hartman at work in Lafontaine studio.

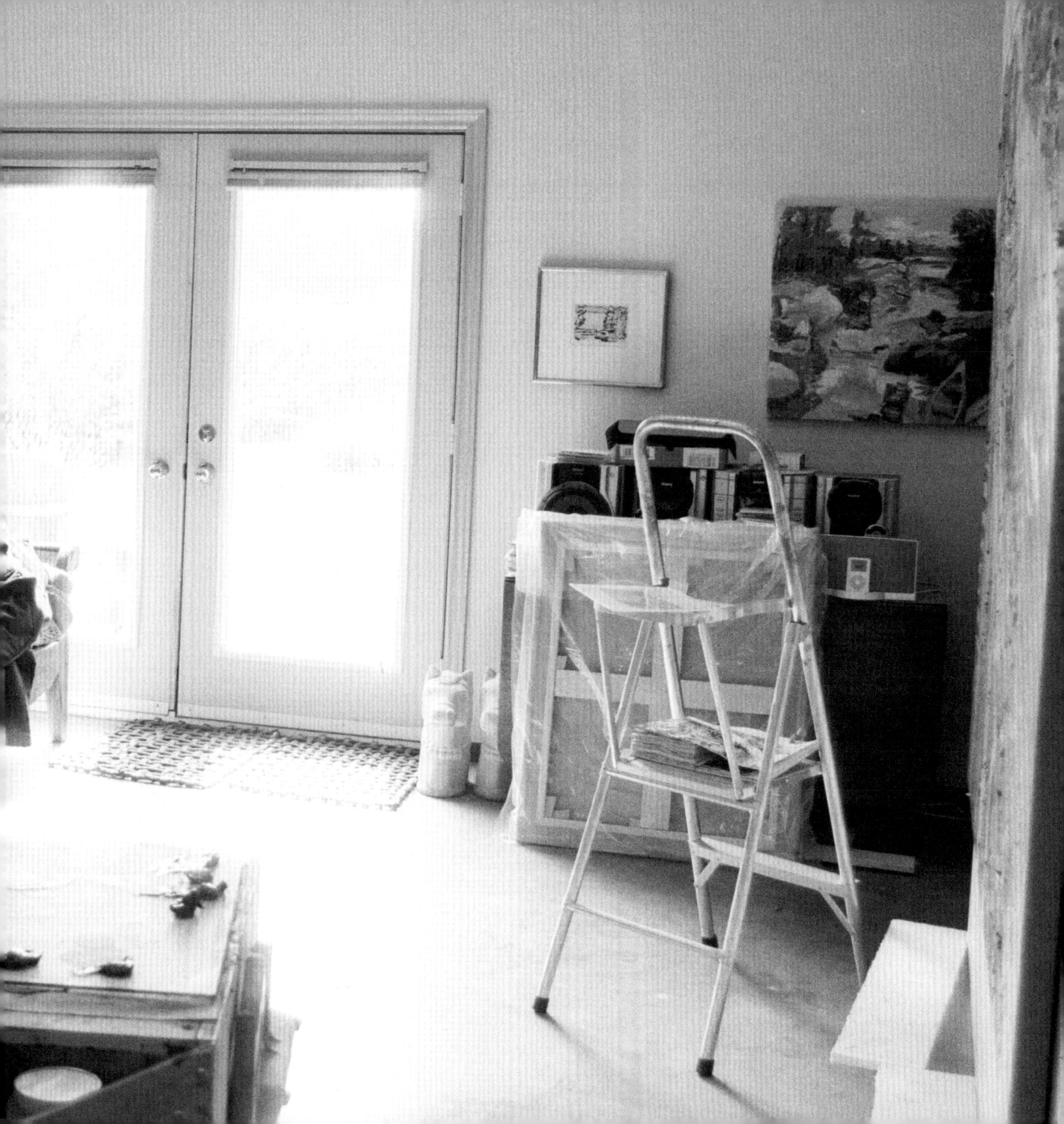

heathers and muddy browns, and the spill of the muddy river into the bottom of the inlet was becoming less distinct and more like effluent. The streets and train tracks were arteries of purple feeding the carbuncular reach of Vancouver's fist upon the shore.

"Does the mood you bring to a painting, perhaps a mood you are not even aware of being in, ever determine more than you would like?"

"Everything is determined by the first stroke," said Hartman, "and then by the first and the second, and after that by the first and the second and the third. If I have an area of a painting that needs fixing, then I like to address it right away by remaining focused and moving forward, because the relationships of all the parts of the painting become more and more complex as I go along, with the result that whatever was my original intention gets sidetracked almost immediately."

At four, Hartman declared that he was done for the day.

"When do you know that a painting is finished?" I asked.

"When all the white is covered up," said Hartman, grinning.

In Hartman's drypoint prints from the late eighties and early nineties, human figures and various narrative elements occupied the celestial regions of his compositions busily—as in *Presbyterian Apocalypse*, a lithograph Hartman created in 1992, in which the painter's grandfather, in a wheelchair, looms over Midland Harbour beside flames with hellish furies in attendance. In certain works from this period, such as *The North Shore* (1989), *Port Severn* (1989), and *Wrecking the Midland Simcoe/Deposition* (1992), there is an indication of the way in which Hartman will use these icons—a church, a demolished grain elevator, or, in *Brébeuf and Lalemant*, a Jesuit martyr on a cross—more sparingly as the landscape itself comes to the fore. In later paintings of Georgian Bay, Newfoundland, and Sept-Îles, for example, the icons that remain tend to be more whimsical—a group of men playing cards, an airplane or helicopter. They mark what is preoccupying Hartman during the work's creation as much as a past he is trying to commemorate. But in the Vancouver paintings, there were none at all.

"Normally," said Hartman, "I would have etched them in and not used some and maybe added others, but it was getting to the point where I was imitating myself and I felt I was doing this because it was expected of me—and that's no good, so I've stopped putting them in. Now I find myself wishing the impulse would come back."

"You've certainly been working more speedily than I expected," I said.

"Painters work more quickly than most people think," said Hartman. "So much to do with painting is about creating the illusion of space. You learn the shortcuts—and to leave out a lot that would otherwise clutter things up."

But in fact the work Hartman does is plenty—and it starts a long time before paint is squeezed from tubes in the studio.

IT BEGINS WITH THE VIEW FROM ON HIGH—but in Halifax Hartman could not find one because a thick, grey cloud was hanging over the city and threatening rain.

It was June, and this was Hartman's second trip to the venerable Canadian Atlantic port city. Prior to his arrival, he had booked a Cessna to fly him over it, but the pilot's prediction of bad weather and insufficient visibility had come to pass. So, instead, we were touring the city at ground level and looking for a building, any building, that might offer a decent vantage point. We drove along the Dartmouth side, and then around the container lands at the north end of the city. Train tracks cut through the silent yards, empty but unbarred for the weekend. The great scaffold pincers that move the containers about were still, and, at the foot of the low bluff on the city side of the yard, a flour mill and its attendant elevators waited for a blast of the siren and the recommencement of work. These bits of industry would probably end up in miniature in the painting Hartman had travelled to Halifax to produce, but his preparations were off to a slow start.

"Halifax is a challenge," said Hartman—his manner gentle and unflappable, as usual. We passed a seafarers' mission and, behind it, a one-room building offering money-wiring services to Filipino crews. "I'll have to draw the city mostly at ground level and that will probably make the place register more completely, but the easiest thing to do would be to find a tall building, wouldn't it?"

Hartman laughed at himself and then was quiet. Fortuitously, a jogger passed and, when we quizzed him, he suggested the offices at 1801 Hollis Street—he knew the building manager, he said, though he warned that as it was the weekend, the office would be closed. Hartman resolved to try the building the next day and, in the meantime, to visit the Halifax Citadel—the British military fort constructed in the mid-eighteenth century, when the Mi'kmaq still roamed the surrounding forests and France was a continental enemy. There he found a point at its northern end from which he was able to look out over Cornwallis Street and the old section of Halifax that lies east of the Common. He unpacked the kit he keeps at hand—the concertina notebook, his

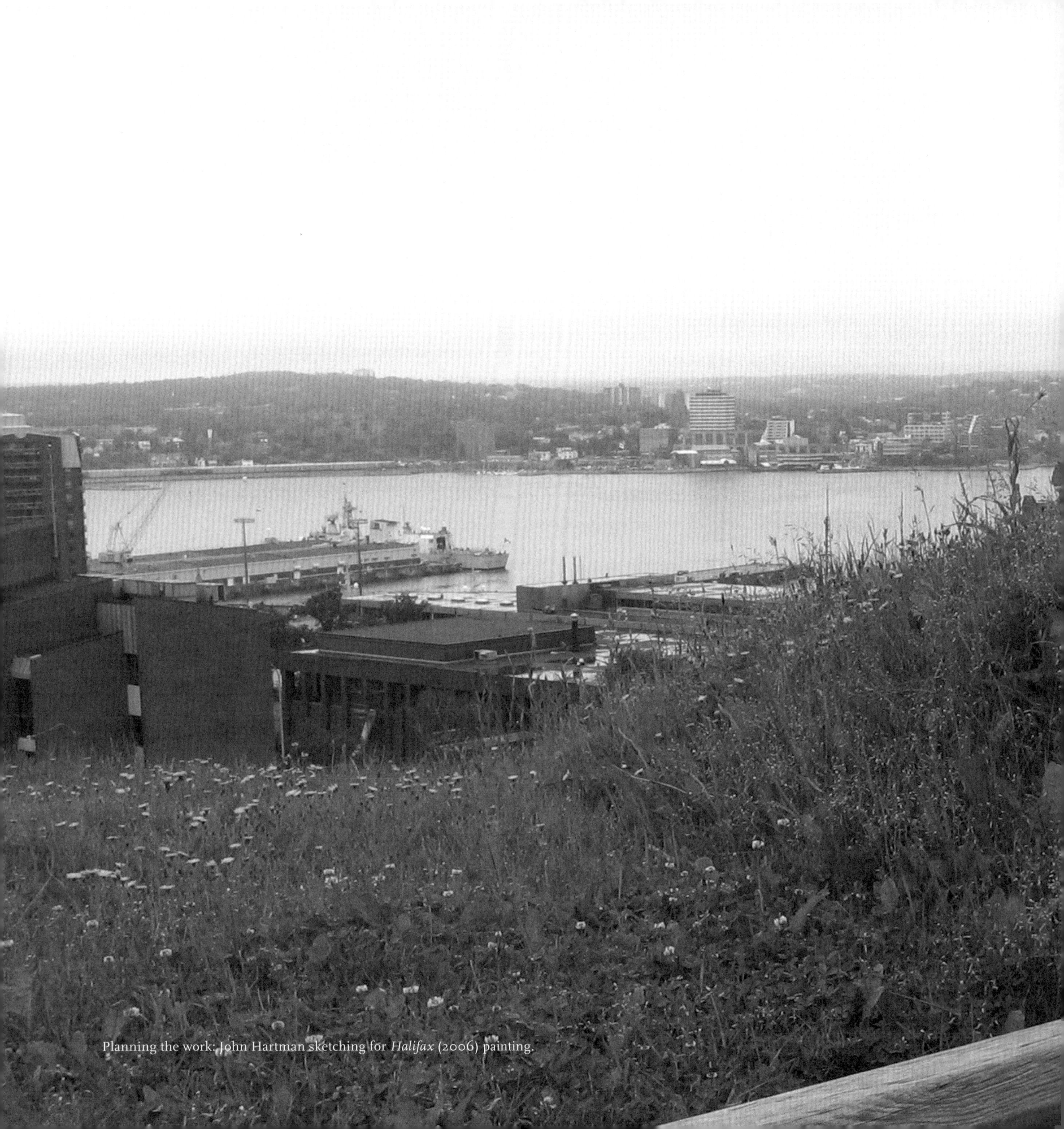

Planning the work: John Hartman sketching for *Halifax* (2006) painting.

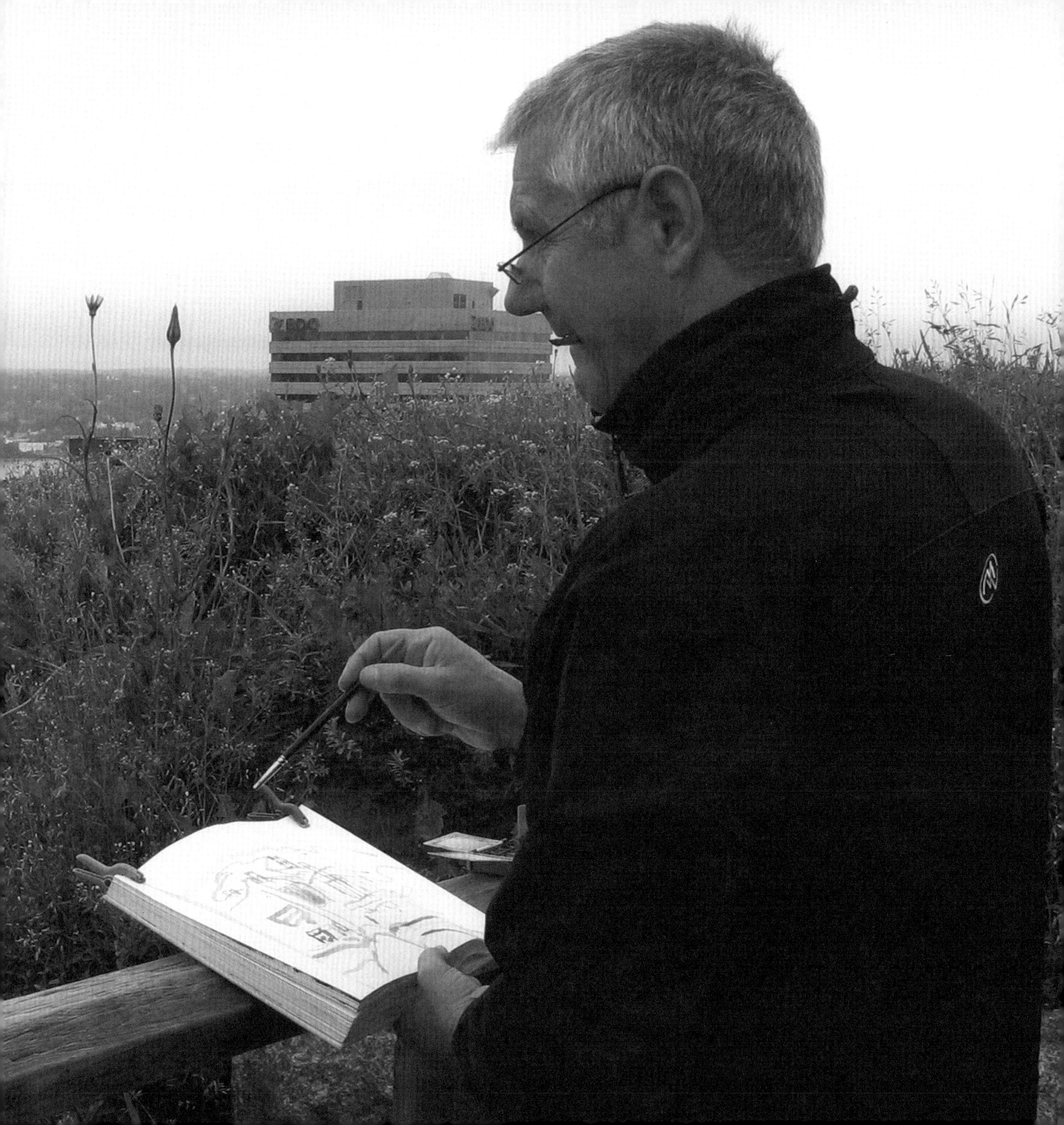

paints, and brushes—and dashed off a quick study of the historic city. I wondered if he was struggling to come to terms with how to paint Halifax. I wondered if he was perhaps still hoping that the Cessna he had booked might take off and lift him above it, or if he was genuinely seeing something unusual and a way into the painting he had planned. At a certain point the spectator must have confidence, because he is only that—an onlooker who must rely on the instincts and ability of an artist that are not his own: *trust*, in other words. It was only me who was worried. It was only me who was lost. Hartman was involved and relying on process—gazing beyond the rampart, his spectacles down upon the tip of his nose again, dabbing quickly and deftly at the notebook's pages with a light brush. There was plenty here for him—lots of colour even on this drab day. Beyond the old city and the docks of the Department of National Defence were the candy-striped stacks of a power plant and the vertical green struts of the Macdonald and MacKay bridges linking Halifax to its companion city of Dartmouth across the Narrows. Streets spun out from the circular road around the citadel and led cars west along Quinpool Road and on to the South Shore or to the Annapolis Valley, but because the overcast sky hid the afternoon sun, it was hard to know where north, south, east, and west were. There was simply Halifax, and there was all around.

"The compass is not clear here," I said.

"No, but there's a general flat light and that's helpful. What's appealing to me is that there is no one dominating point of organization in the city. There are so many *pulls* here. The complexity of painting Halifax arises out of the fact of there being water on all sides and of the land being quite high in places. All this makes the city attractive—but also harder to figure out."

The next day, at 1801 Hollis Street, we were led without fuss up the service stairs to the top of the several-storey building. The view from the flat rooftop was unimpeded—though, in truth, we were not terribly high. Hartman professed interest in the activity along the near side of the harbour, where the grey vessels of the Canadian Forces were moored the length of Barrington Street, a busy road that leads out towards the MacKay Bridge and the highway north to Bedford. (A painting would be born of that scene later.) In the other direction was McNabs Island, then Purcell's Cove and the Atlantic. Hartman took photographs from all four sides of the building, though he did not bring out his notebook on this occasion; it was not clear to me if he was particularly inspired or merely making the best of a problematic situation.

A tall ship and then a container vessel made their way in from the sea, past the market, pubs, hotels, and nightclubs along Hollis and Lower Water Street.

"Finding a suitable vantage point must have been so much easier in Manhattan," I said.

Beyond whatever the eye perceives and below the well of personal memory is a deeper fount of societal reminiscences.

Hartman shrugged and took another photograph.

"Often, I think that I paint in much the same way that the cartographers of the nineteenth century created maps," said Hartman. "I find myself surveying and working *around* an idea and only afterwards imagining the site from on high. If I am able to rely on photographs, then my work tends to be more realistic—or at least parts of the paintings are—but for this one I'm going to need to rely on memory a lot more, and although it will take a while to figure out what I'll be trying to do in the studio, *not* flying may actually produce a better painting in the end."

Beyond whatever the eye perceives and below the well of personal memory is a deeper fount of societal reminiscences. In the Halifax painting—as he had done in the *Wendake* paintings of Midland and the land around Georgian Bay (though not in his paintings of Vancouver, where the shock of the new city had thrust the sensibility of the painting entirely into the present)—these atavistic memories would surface in narrative iconic elements, again. The turning point for the city—its terrible defining moment—was the Halifax Explosion of December sixth, 1917, when the *Mont-Blanc*, a French munitions ship, and the *Imo*, a Norwegian vessel carrying Belgian relief supplies, collided in the narrowest part of the harbour. Most of the northern end of the city was razed, the explosion carrying such force that the anchor shaft of the *Mont-Blanc* was blown more than two kilometres from the Narrows, all the way up the Northwest Arm. One of the ship's guns was hurled the length of the harbour and into Dartmouth. Some two thousand people were killed, nine thousand left homeless, and ten thousand injured.

The Halifax Explosion was the biggest single detonation of man-made materials before Hiroshima. It was the subject of the Montreal writer Hugh MacLennan's first novel, *Barometer Rising* (1941), and it has been remembered in a number of histories, including Laura M. Mac Donald's *Curse of the Narrows*, but its devastation is not known to have been recorded in oil paint by any Canadian artist working in Halifax at the time. At the Art Gallery of Nova Scotia there are paintings by A. Y. Jackson depicting the harbour and the First World War fleet that often crowded the Narrows, but none of the aftermath of the explosion. And although Jackson's Group of Seven colleague Arthur Lismer made many sketches of the devastation, and one known watercolour, *Sorrow*, neither painter ever made it the subject of a more significant work.

"But I can understand that," said Hartman. "If I had been in New York in September, 2001, it would have taken me a lot of time to have been able to paint anything to do with 9/11."

Lack, of course, is an explicit invitation to an artist. Later, in his Lafontaine studio, Hartman would resurrect the Halifax Explosion of 1917 by commemorating it in a clever variation on the oppressive cloud that hung over the city during our visit. In *Halifax*, the finished painting, the thick wet mist that had ruled out Hartman's airplane ride had morphed into a billowing explosion of ash and debris. In it, and the surrounding sky, Hartman had made brusque sketches of iconic objects—brushes with the city's memory, effectively. The action in the ash cloud and sky hangs over the city much like Altdorfer's banner, Hartman's icons telling the story of the city just as the Renaissance painter's Latin words did the Battle of Issus.

"I'd been trying to understand the explosion and the area it affected through street names," said Hartman as we both considered the 96-by-198-inch triptych. The smaller painting of Barrington Street, *1801 Hollis*, was propped up against the wall beside it.

"I had a dotted line that I had drawn, basically between the two bridges," said Hartman, "but the painting was too neat. Then I found an old photograph of the explosion and I realized that I could put the mushroom cloud over the citadel and that it would connect the two bridges in a triangle. I think that it became a much stronger composition that way."

"And where did all the red come from?" I said. "That's not what I remember seeing."

"The pastel study had been all greens and browns and blacks," said Hartman, "but when you start you make certain decisions about colour and light and these decisions precipitate the colours that ensue. I wanted to do a painting that had a grey, overcast sky and so the first thing that I painted was the water, but I'd also decided that the water was going to have a fairly light tone and everything flowed from that."

"And I see that your icons have returned," I said. "This flotilla in the Narrows is obviously a reference to the war."

"That's right," said Hartman. "In the middle of the cloud is the engine room of a corvette. I have it there because my father was a stoker in one during the Second World War. There's the anchor shaft that was thrown out of the harbour, and the plane to the right of it is a reference to Swissair Flight 111, which went down over Peggy's Cove—so, yes, there are icons and all sorts of time frames in the painting."

"Does *Halifax* remind you of your Jesuit paintings at all?"

"Yes, although this painting is more unusual as there's a lot more drawing in it. In the earlier ones, you have more parts that are purely painting. I realize, of course, that what I do is highly subjective and that what I choose to capture reflects my own take on the place, but now what I find exciting is the possibility that someone might be able to point and say, 'This is the MacKay Bridge and this is where I grew up'—"

"So that they are pointing into the thing you've imagined but seeing something real—they're pointing into that idea, really."

"Somebody did it a couple of days ago."

"It's a kind of psycho-geography, really."

"Yes. I want the painting to be a map, though obviously not quite the same as a map."

JULY 2006, NORTH OF BYNG INLET, ON GEORGIAN BAY. Hartman has taken his wife, Trish, his daughter Catherine, my wife Sarah Maclachlan and me along for a day's painting.

"I like being out here," said Hartman. "The painting I do here is of a much more naturalistic kind. It's a way of celebrating being here."

The granite islands here are low and flat and worn. The rocks are dispersed along the edge of the bay and are bleached orange and pink and red, the grain of them like the rings of petrified trees from some primordial age. The stunted trees that do manage to grow here—pine and scrub oak mostly—are wily and bend with the wind. The broad clumps of weather-beaten rock resemble the bellies of whales risen to the water's surface and rolling on their backs to take in the sun. This is what the world will look like after a flood, I thought.

Hartman has erected his easel and is painting the scene on a small piece of board. The light is brilliant, gentle, and clear. There is, even on the board on which he is working, the sense of a world stretching away.

"I foolishly thought I could go on painting this region my whole life," said Hartman.

"There are enough islands," I said. "It would be obsessive, but you could."

"When I was a kid," said Hartman, "I always dreamed of flying. I had this ability to imagine the ground as a film—to see the Earth as a moving picture rolling towards me at an oblique angle. Now, because I am able to gather the information, I can do that."

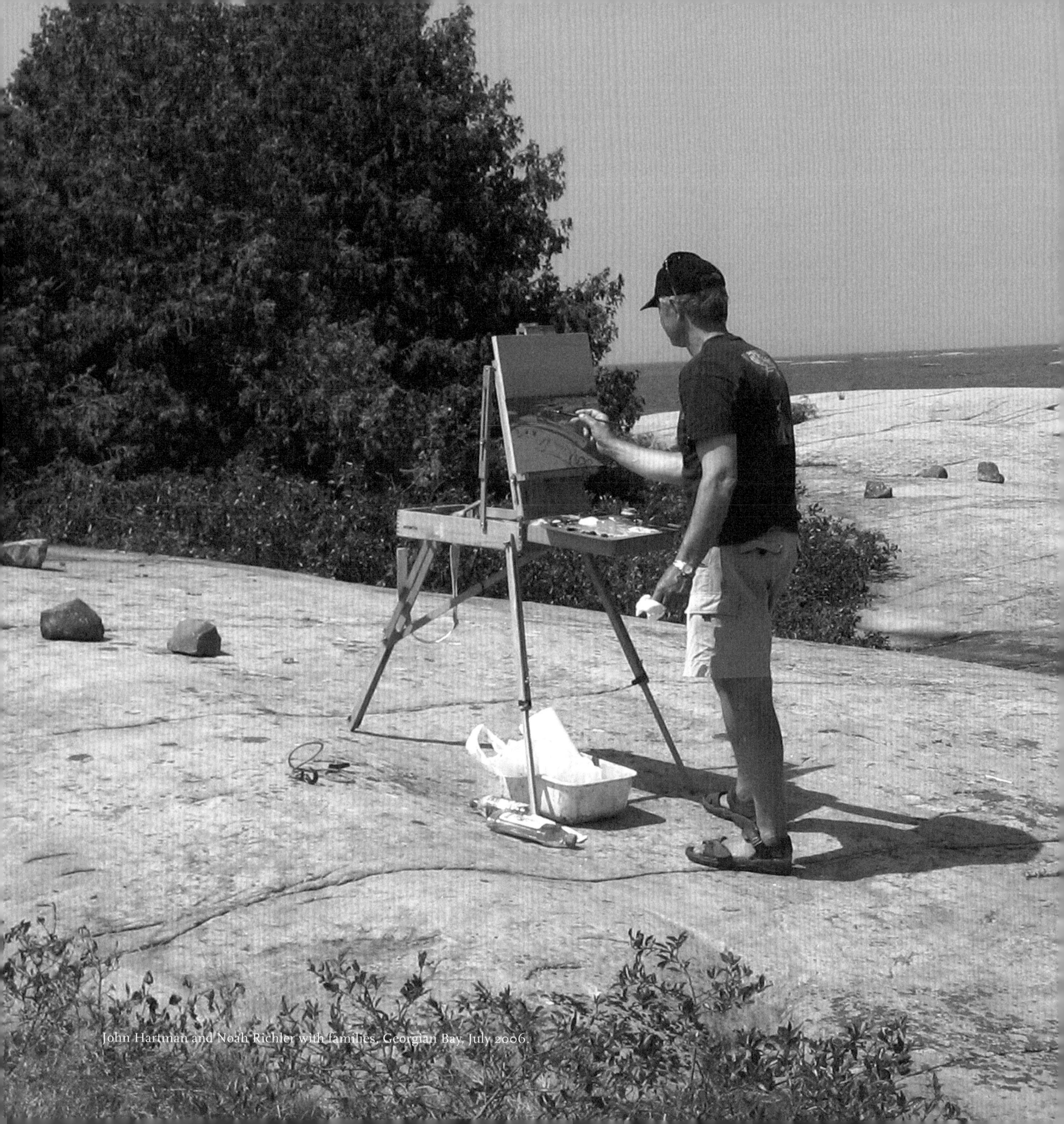

John Hartman and Noah Richler with families, Georgian Bay, July 2006.

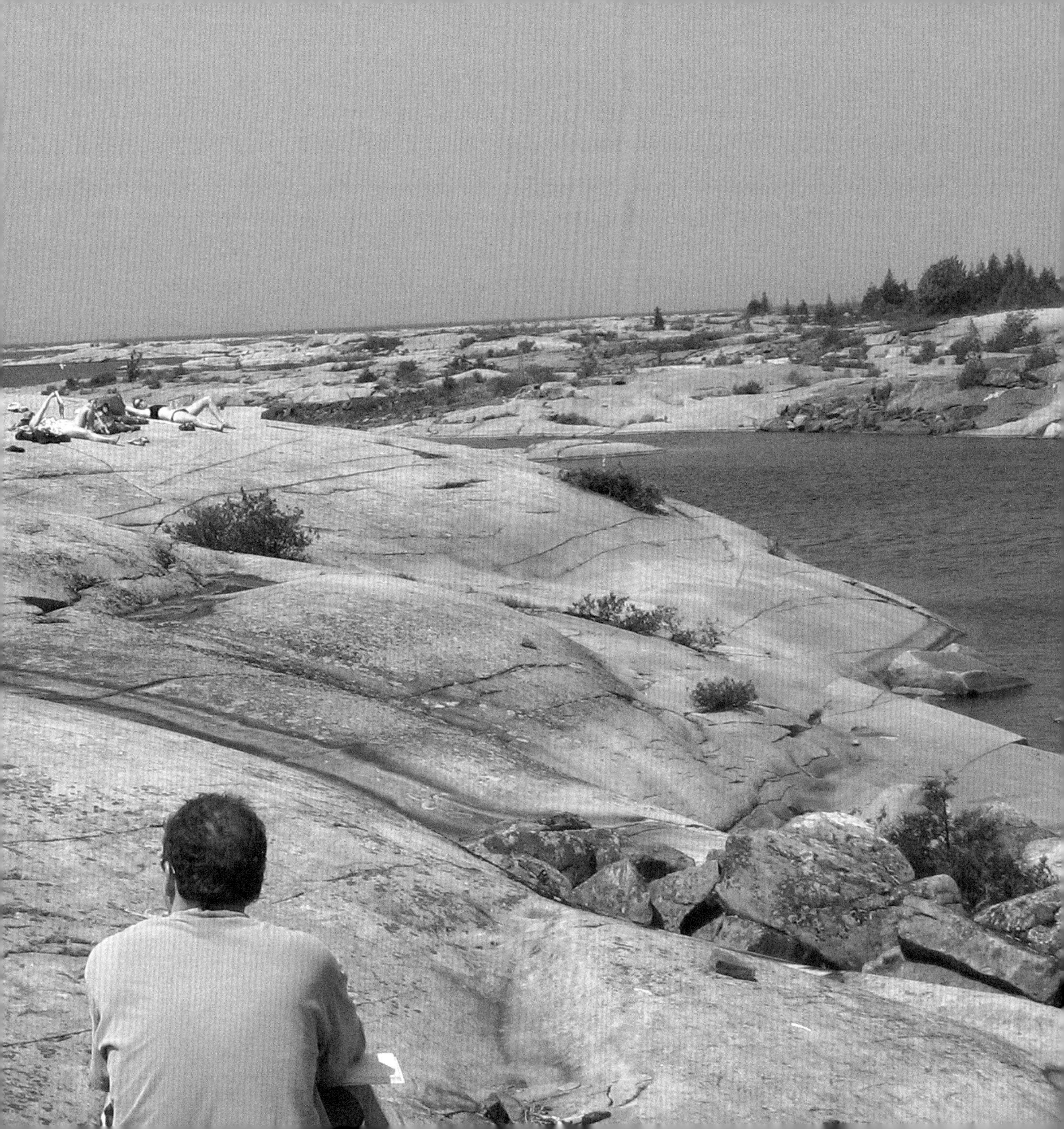

But John Hartman has always had that information. A part of him has always been in the air, observing the land—this territory, his first place—from the oblique overhead angles that he finds so compelling. This land from Huronia to Georgian Bay, the southern reach of the Laurentian Shield, provided Hartman with his first artist's invitation—and offers a key to understanding the emphatic line that can be drawn from his early drypoint prints through the landscapes of Newfoundland to the paintings that he was presently doing of cities.

The land here is devoid of anything high. Altitude is not the issue. Merely standing up, one has the sensation of being tall. Breadth is the insuperable dimension. The impossible, humbling *width* of things is the land's daunting feature. To cross the world as Hartman does—to soar over the land to its very horizon—is the delirious, beautiful act.

NOAH RICHLER is an award-winning journalist and author of *This Is My Country, What's Yours? A Literary Atlas of Canada* (McClelland & Stewart, 2006).

CITIES JOHN HARTMAN

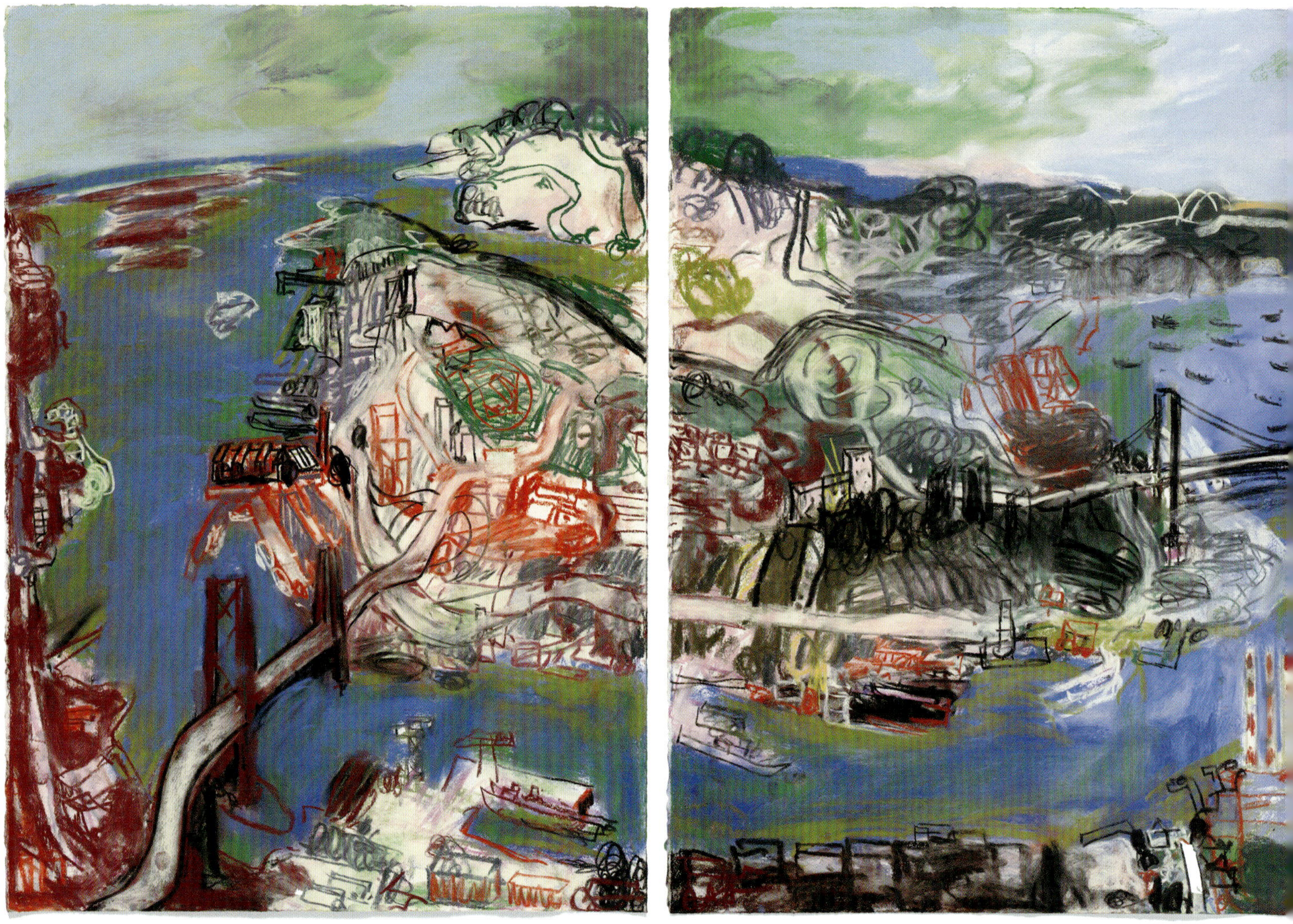

HALIFAX
2006
Pastel on paper
76 x 164 cm (30 x 64.5 inches), triptych

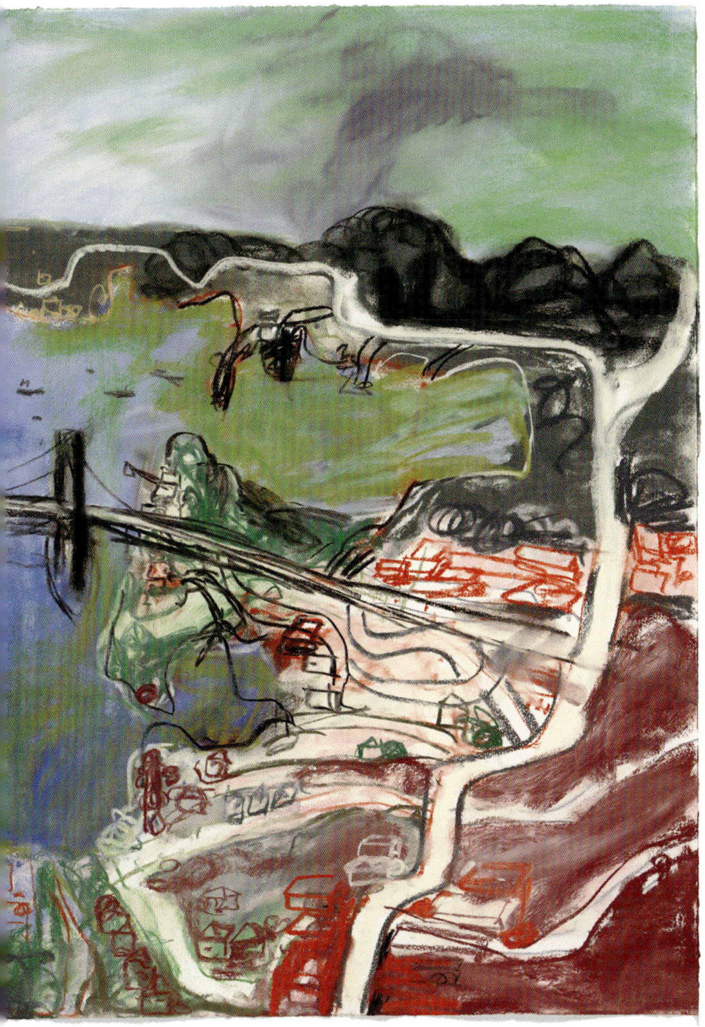

overleaf
HALIFAX
2006
Oil on linen
244 x 503 cm (96 x 198 inches), triptych

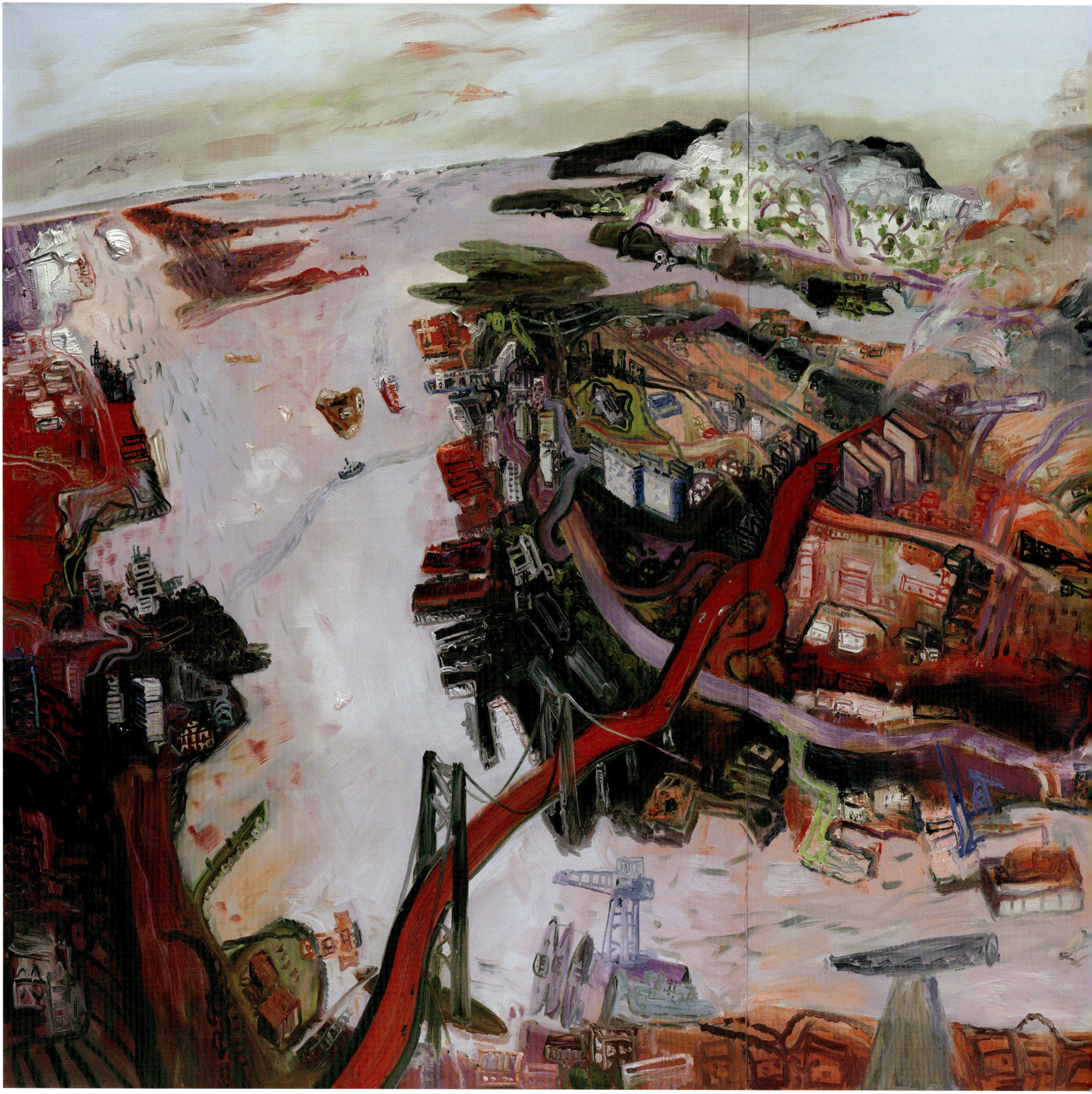

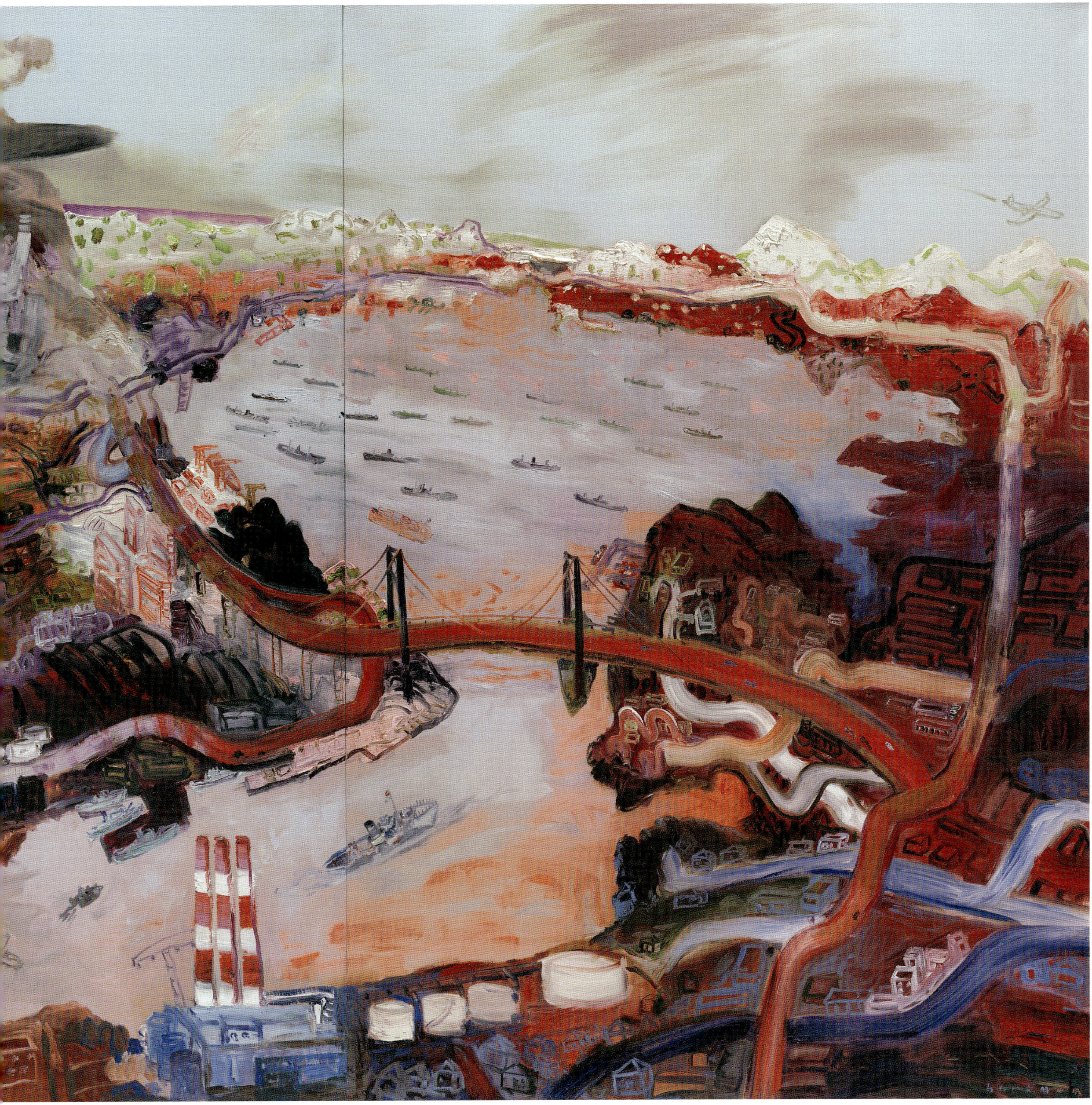

THE NARROWS
2006
Oil on linen
152 x 168 cm (60 x 66 inches)

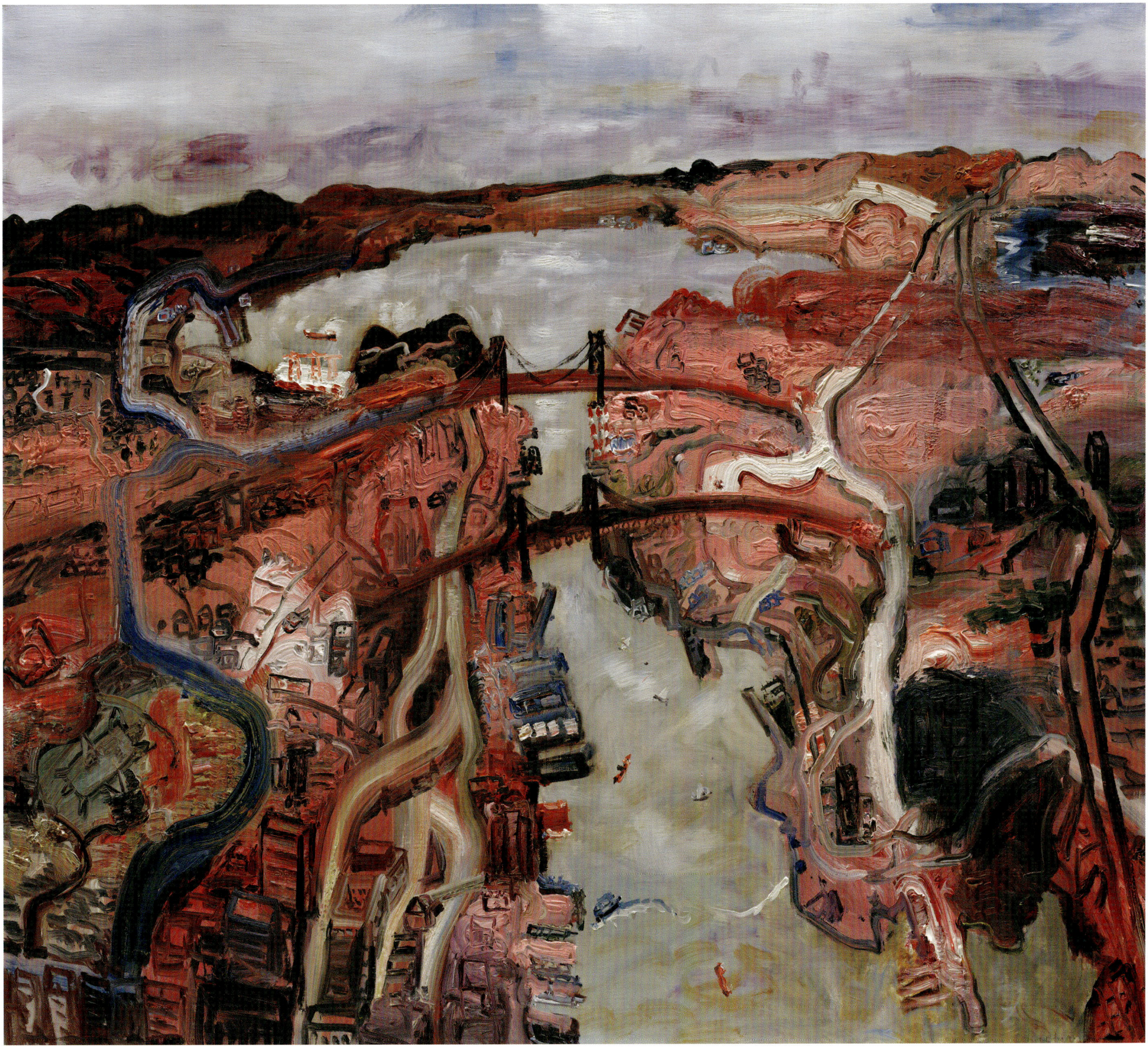

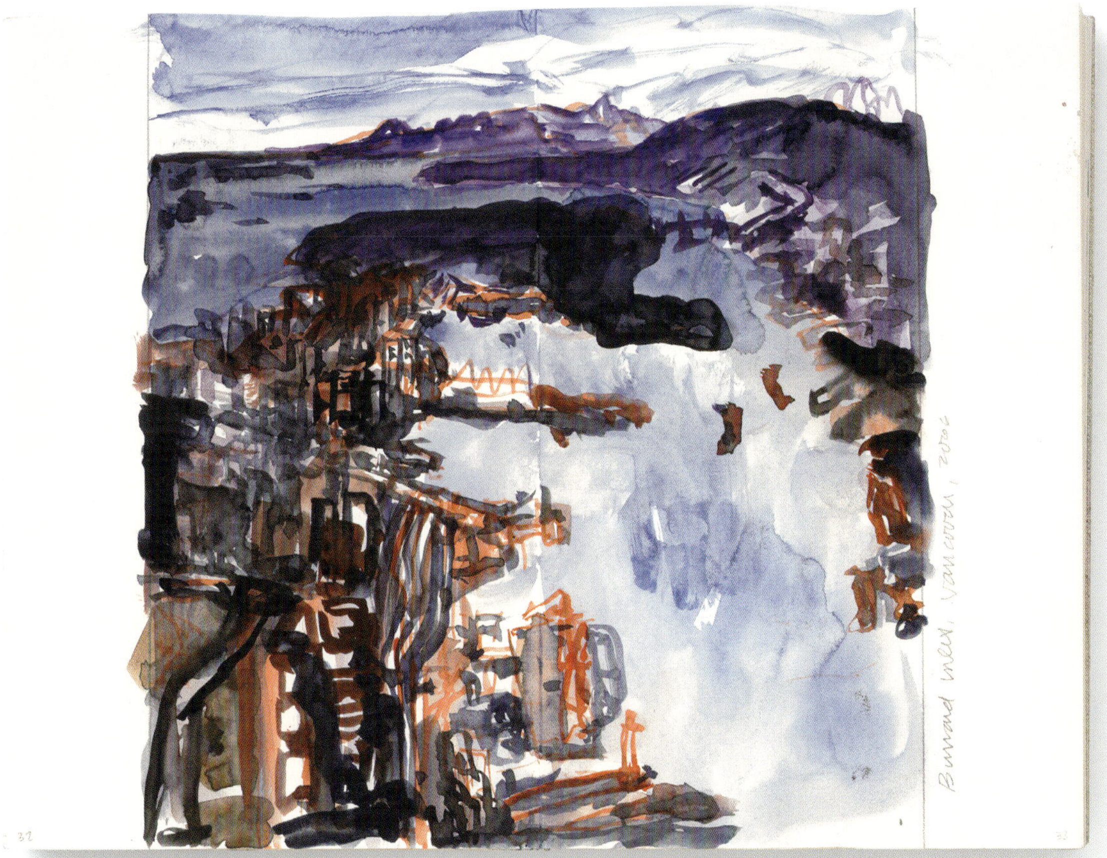

BURRARD INLET, VANCOUVER
2006
Watercolour and graphite on paper; Concertina folding sketchbook 1, pp. 32–33, bound paper, 138 pages
24 x 17 cm (9.5 x 6.5 inches), folded

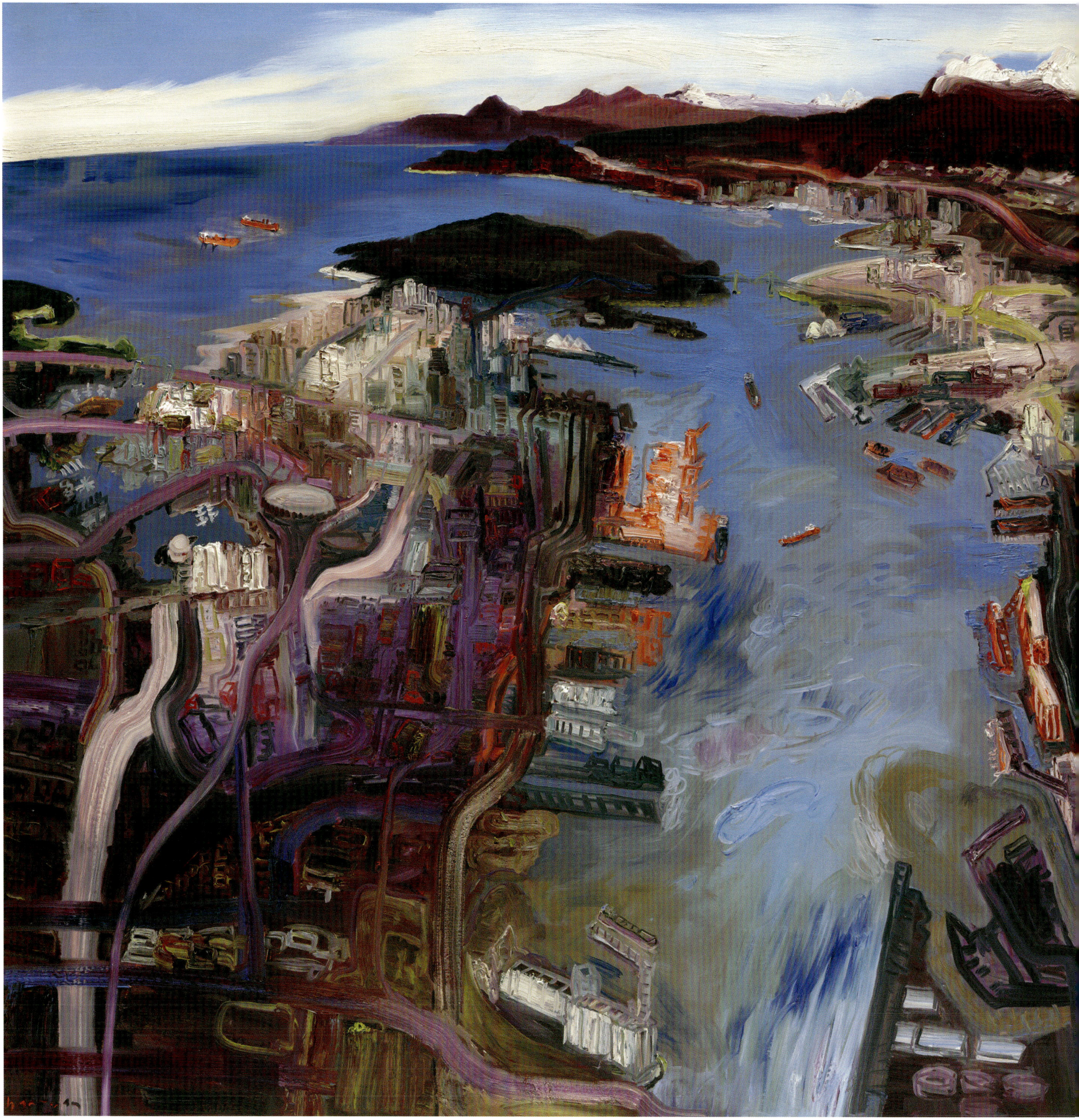

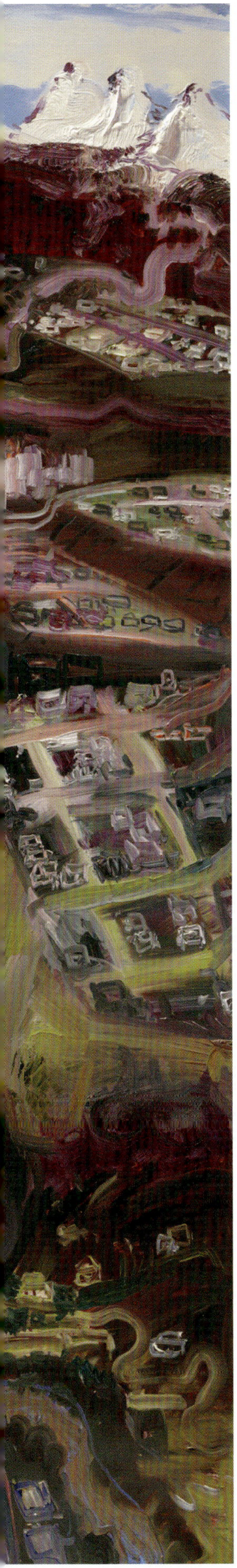

VANCOUVER FROM ABOVE BURRARD INLET
2006
Oil on linen
198 x 229 cm (78 x 90 inches)

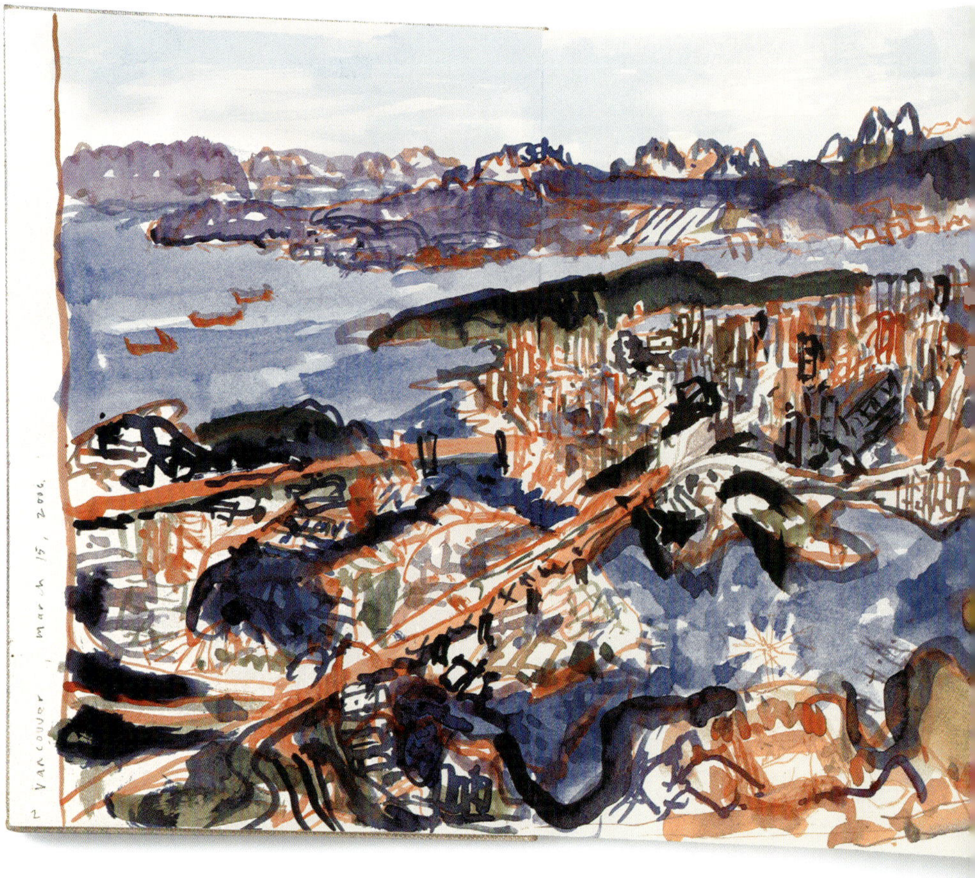

VANCOUVER
2006
Watercolour and graphite on paper; Concertina folding sketchbook 1, pp. 2–5, bound paper, 138 pages
24 x 17 cm (9.5 x 6.5 inches), folded

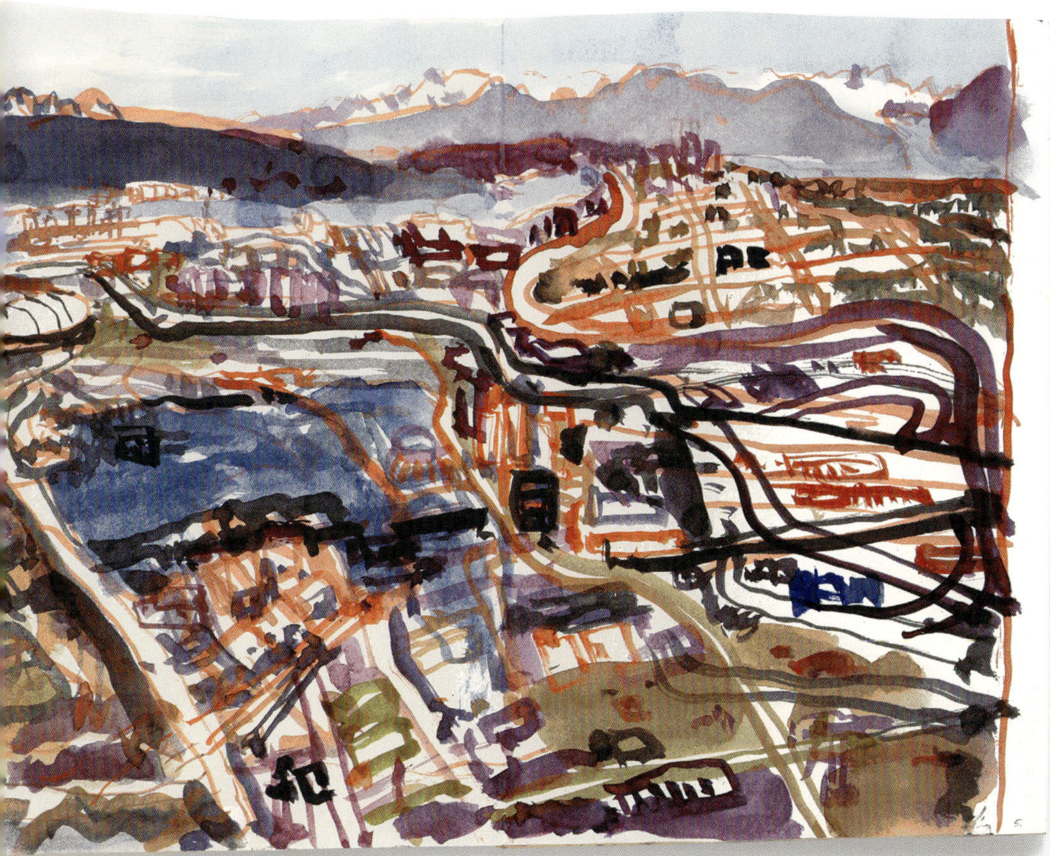

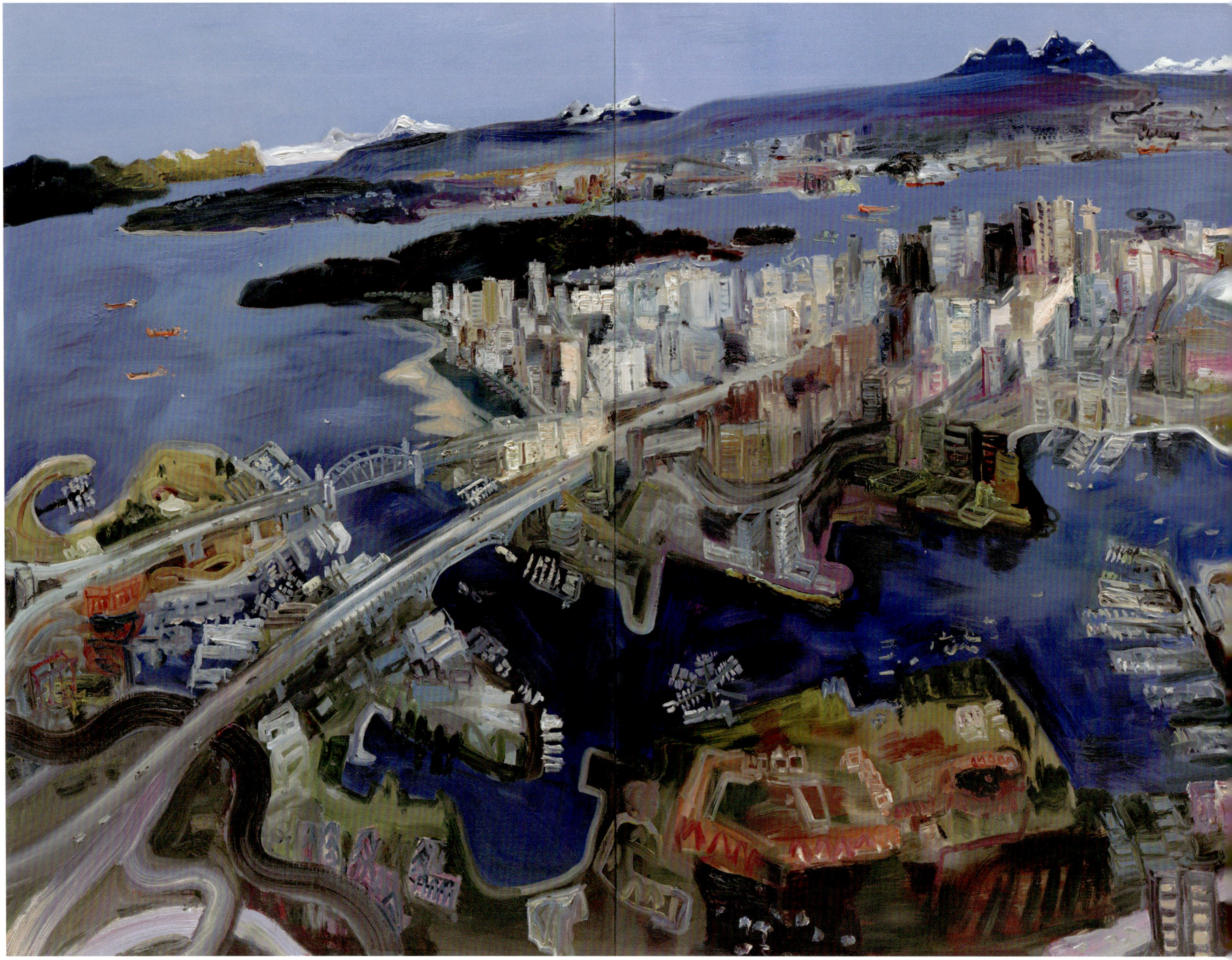

VANCOUVER
2006
Oil on linen
168 x 552 cm (66 x 172 inches), triptych

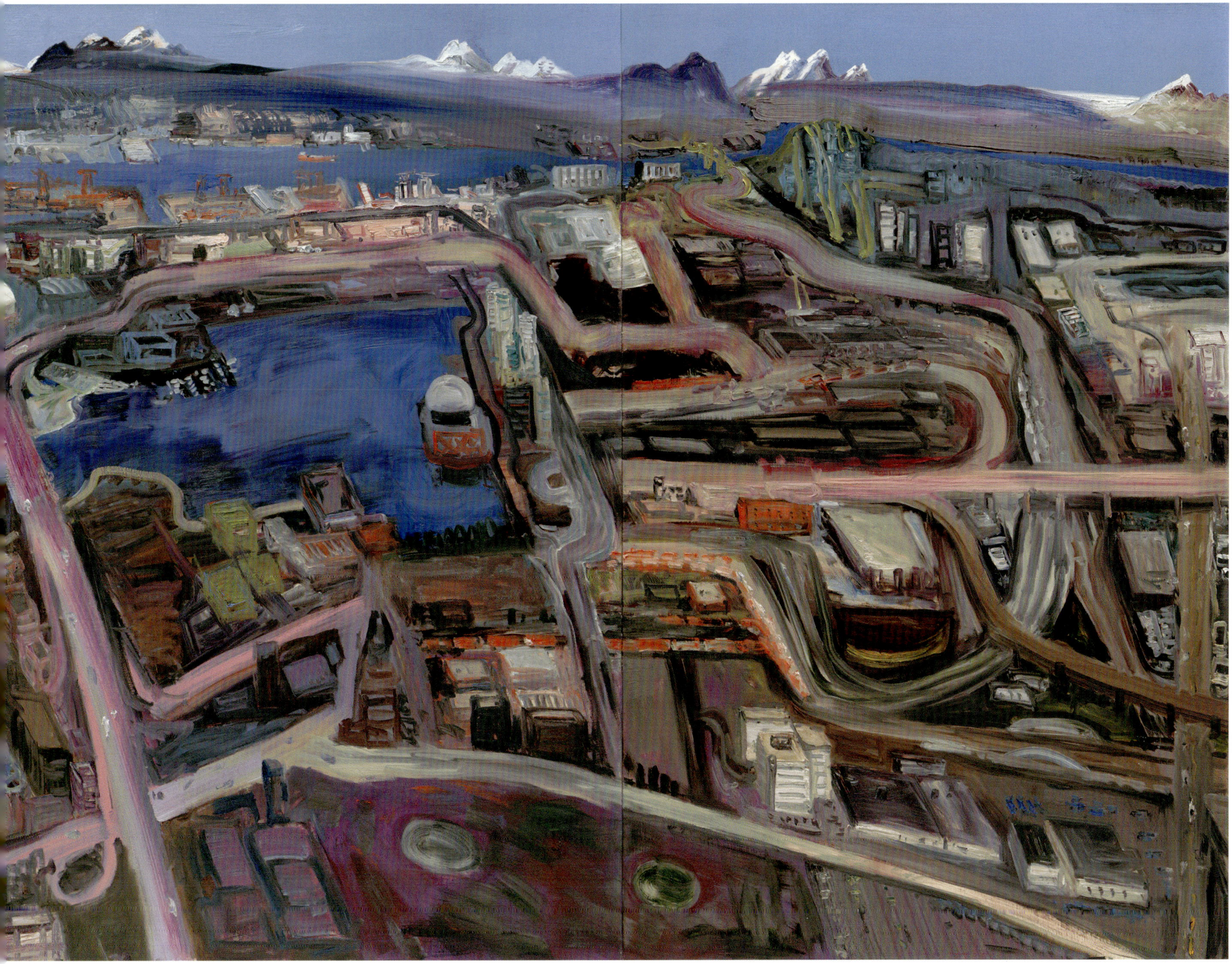

BURRARD INLET
2006
Oil on linen
122 x 137 cm (48 x 54 inches)

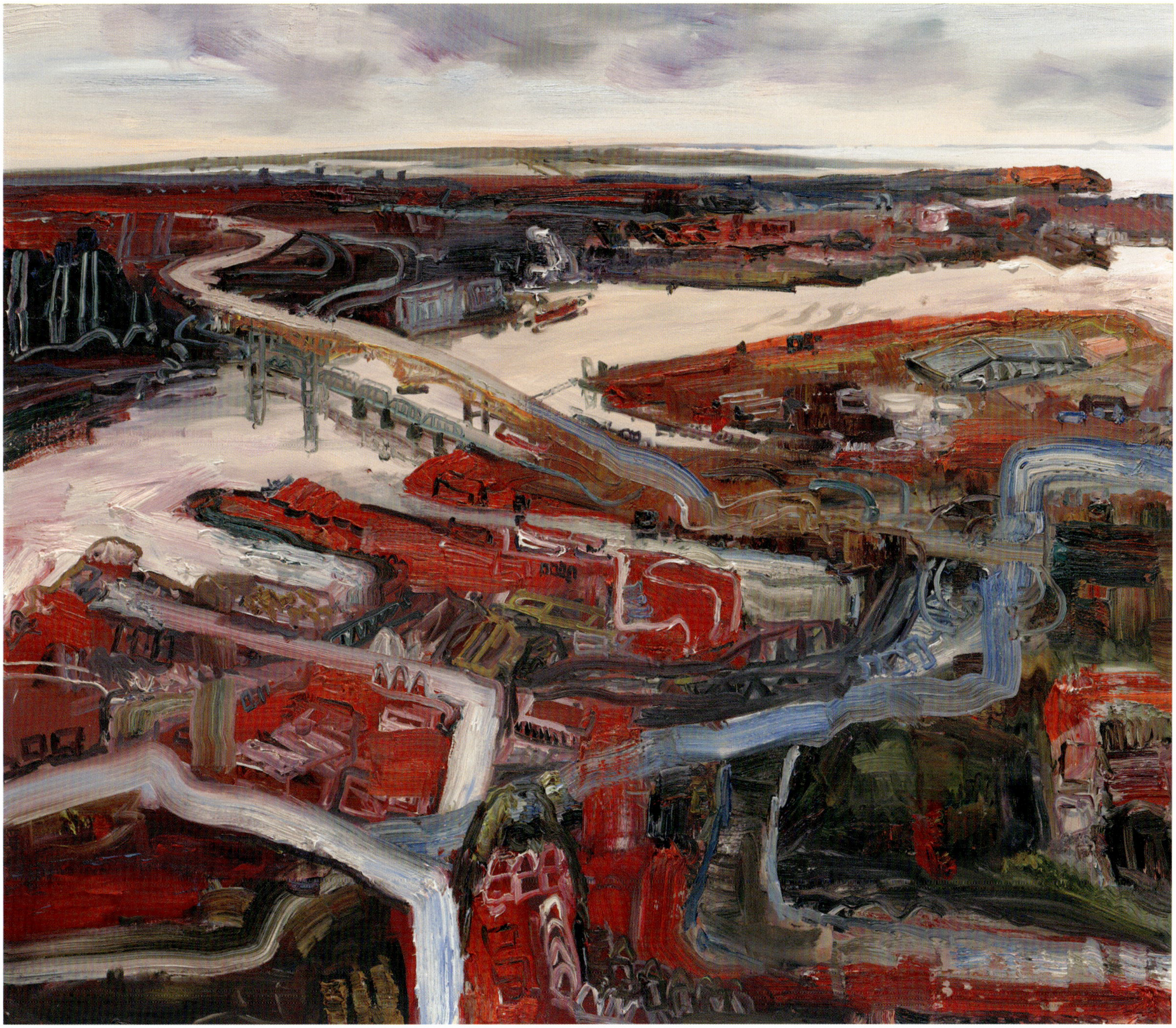

CALGARY
2005
Oil on linen
152 x 168 cm (60 x 66 inches)

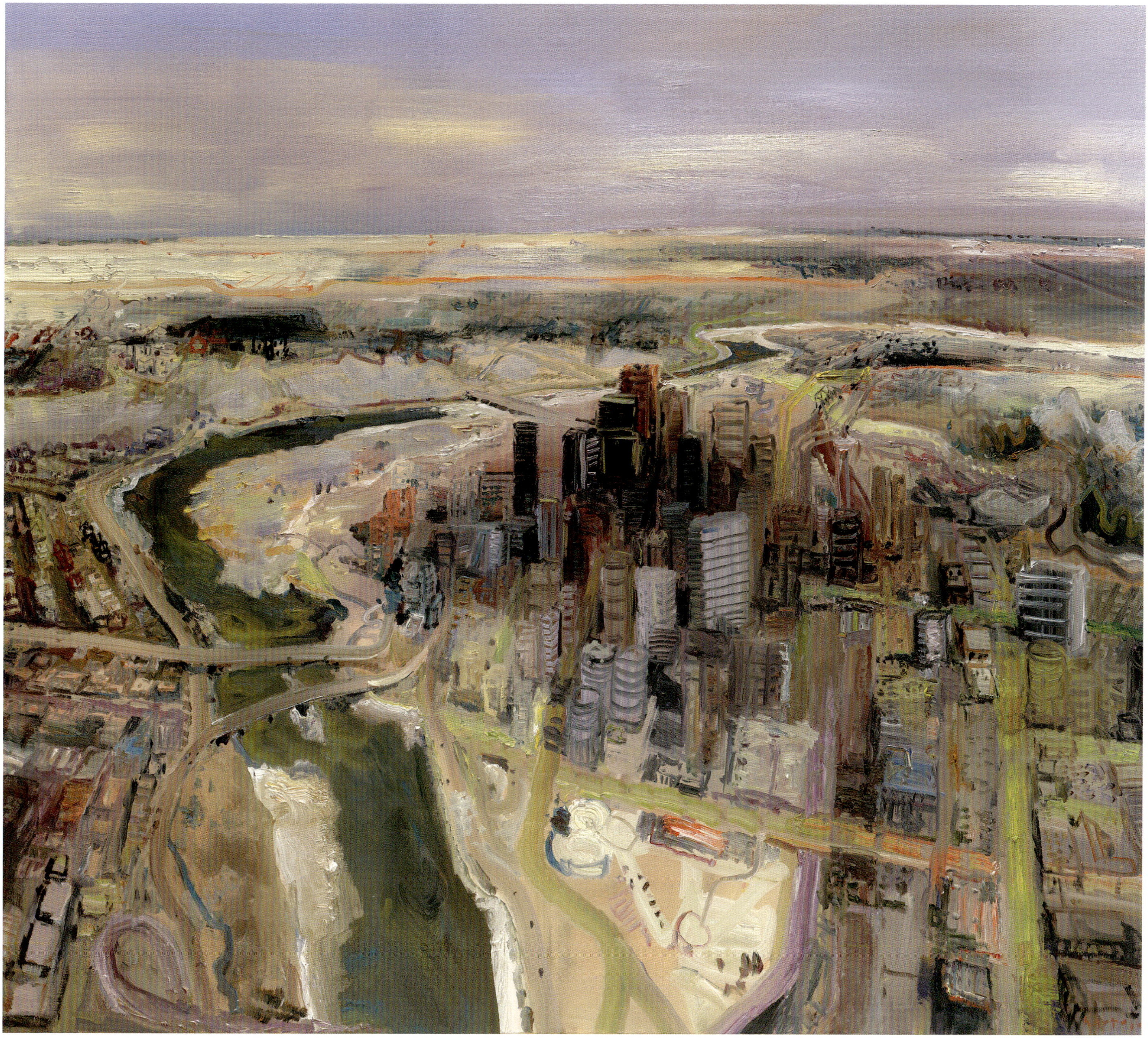

HAMILTON HARBOUR FROM ABOVE

2004

Oil on linen

152 x 168 cm (60 x 66 inches)

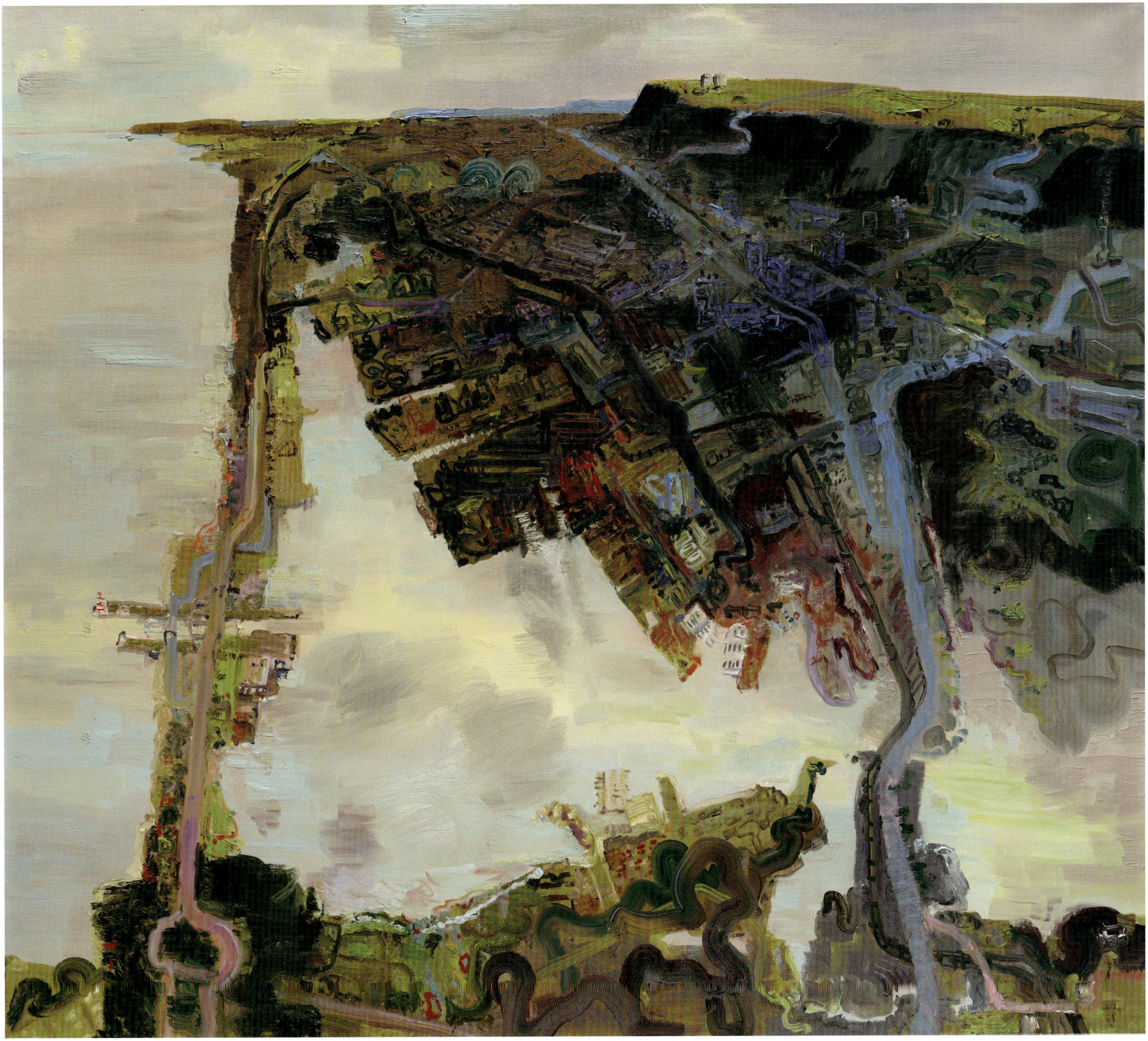

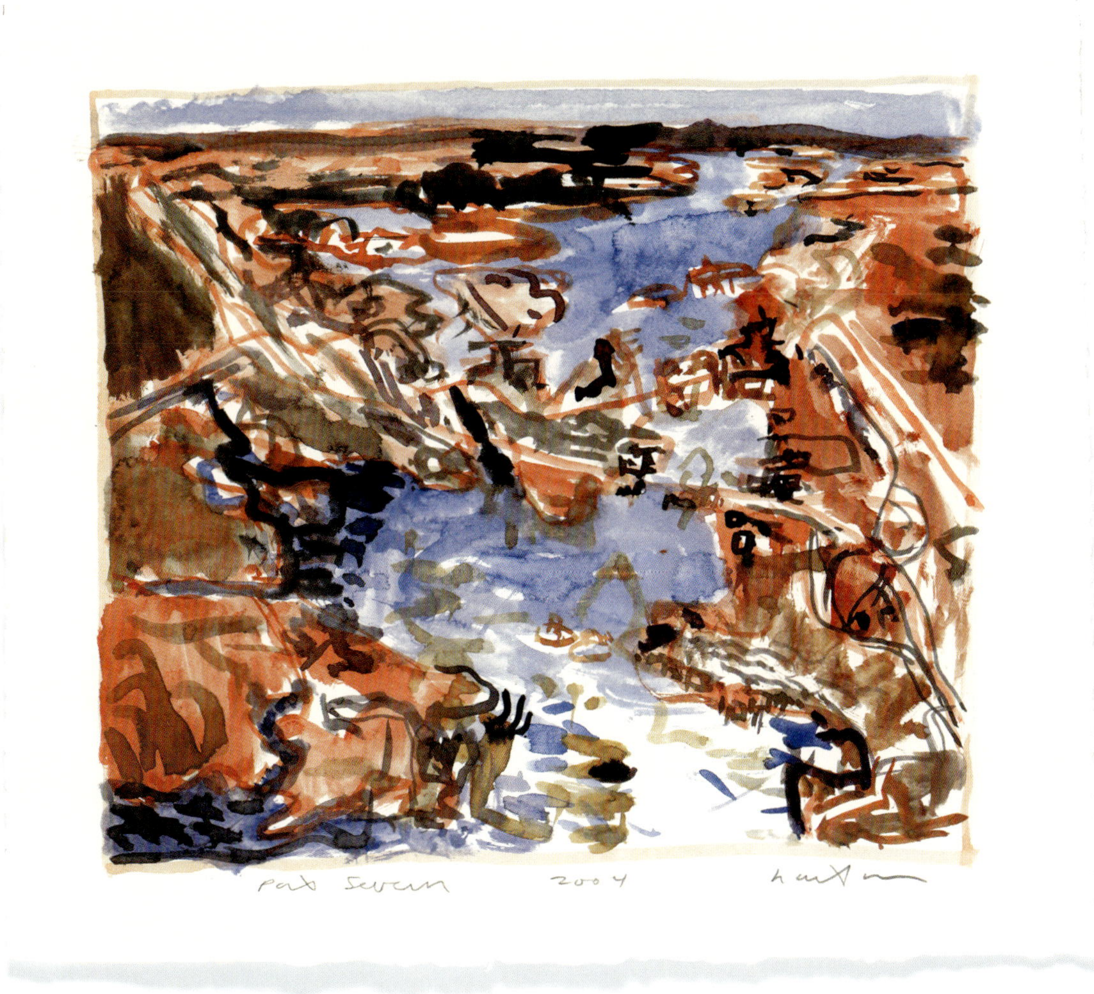

PORT SEVERN

2004

Watercolour on paper

28.5 x 38 cm (11.25 x 15 inches)

PORT SEVERN
2004
Oil on linen
152 x 168 cm (60 x 66 inches)

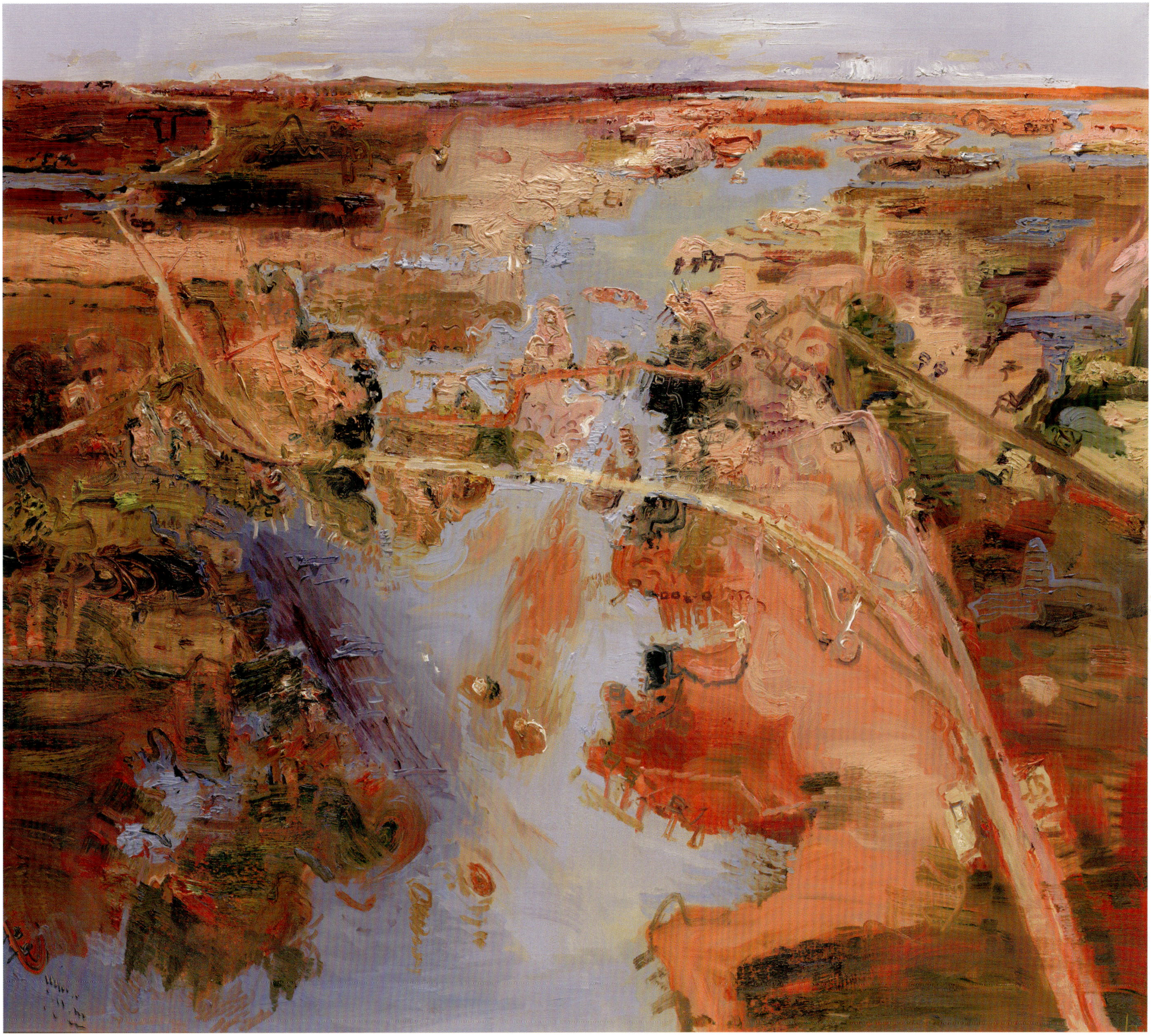

PARRY SOUND

2003

Oil on linen

203 x 196 cm (80 x 77 inches)

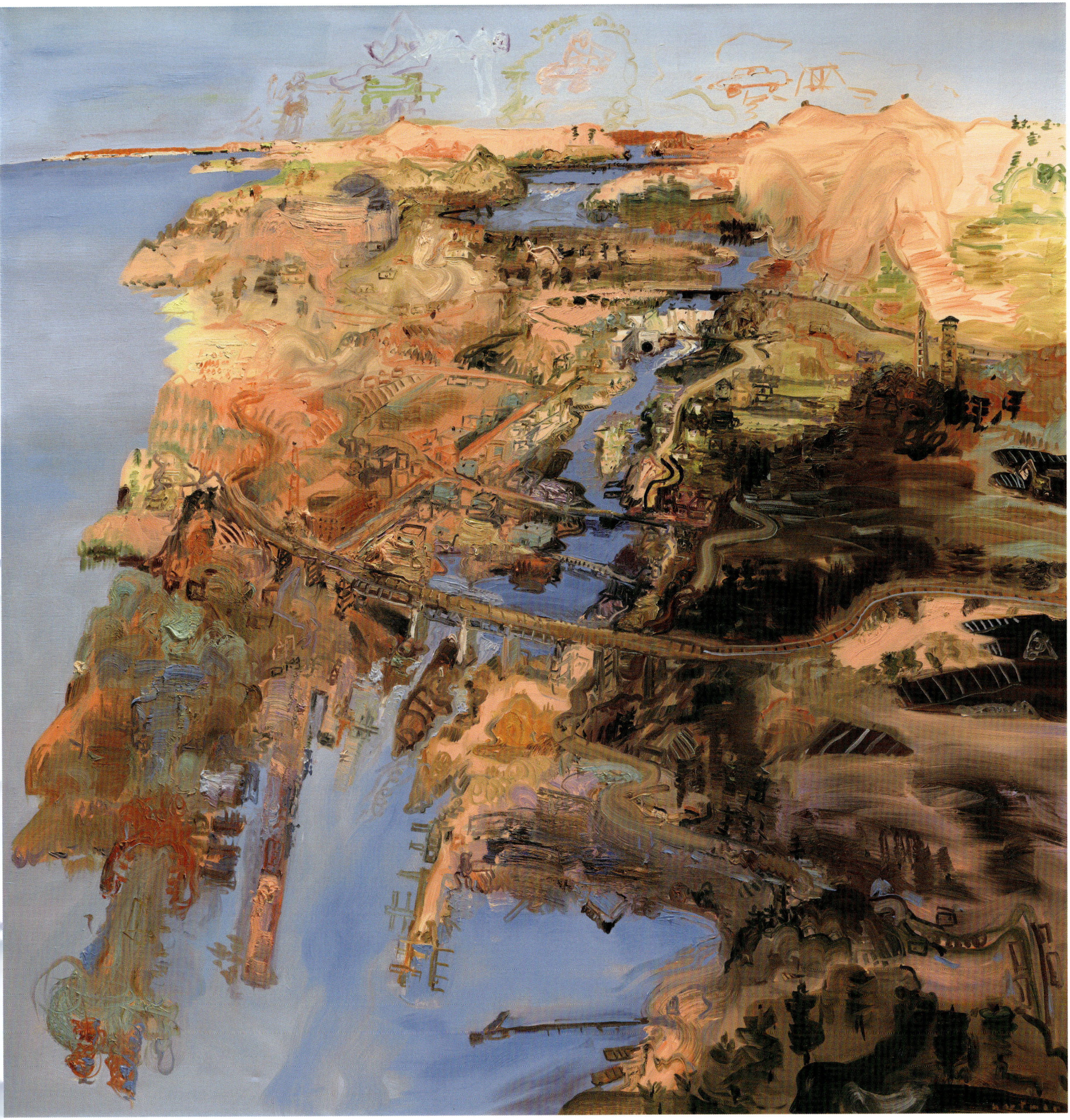

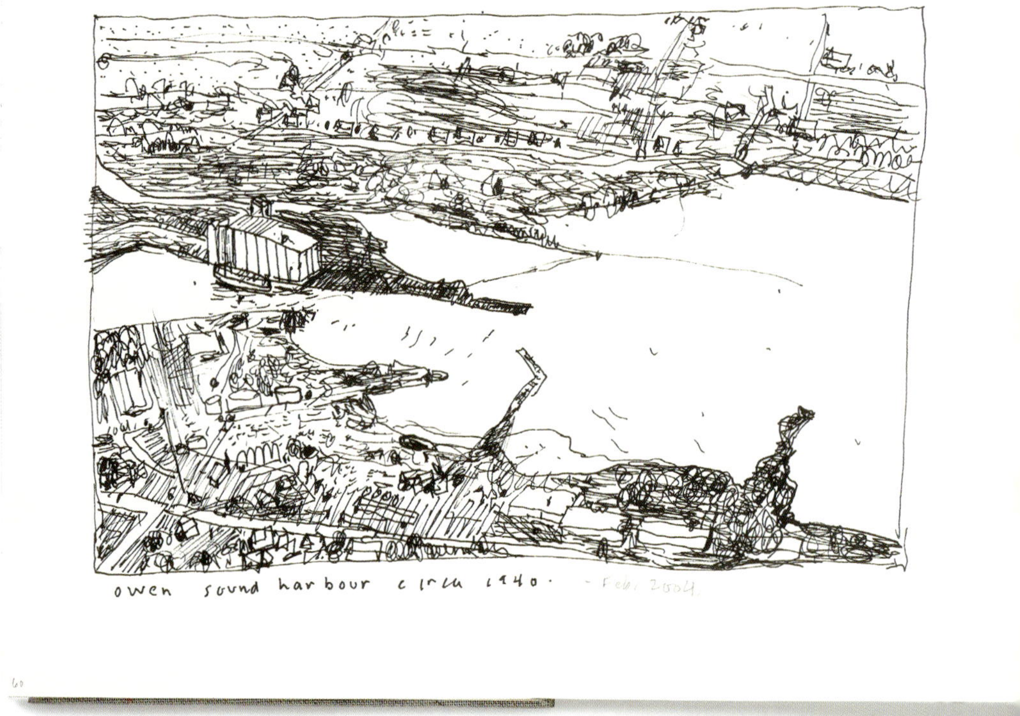

OWEN SOUND HARBOUR, c. 1940 and WINTER BERTHS, OWEN SOUND
2004
Ink on paper; Concertina folding sketchbook 4, pp. 60–63, bound paper, 138 pages
24 x 17 cm (9.5 x 6.5 inches), folded

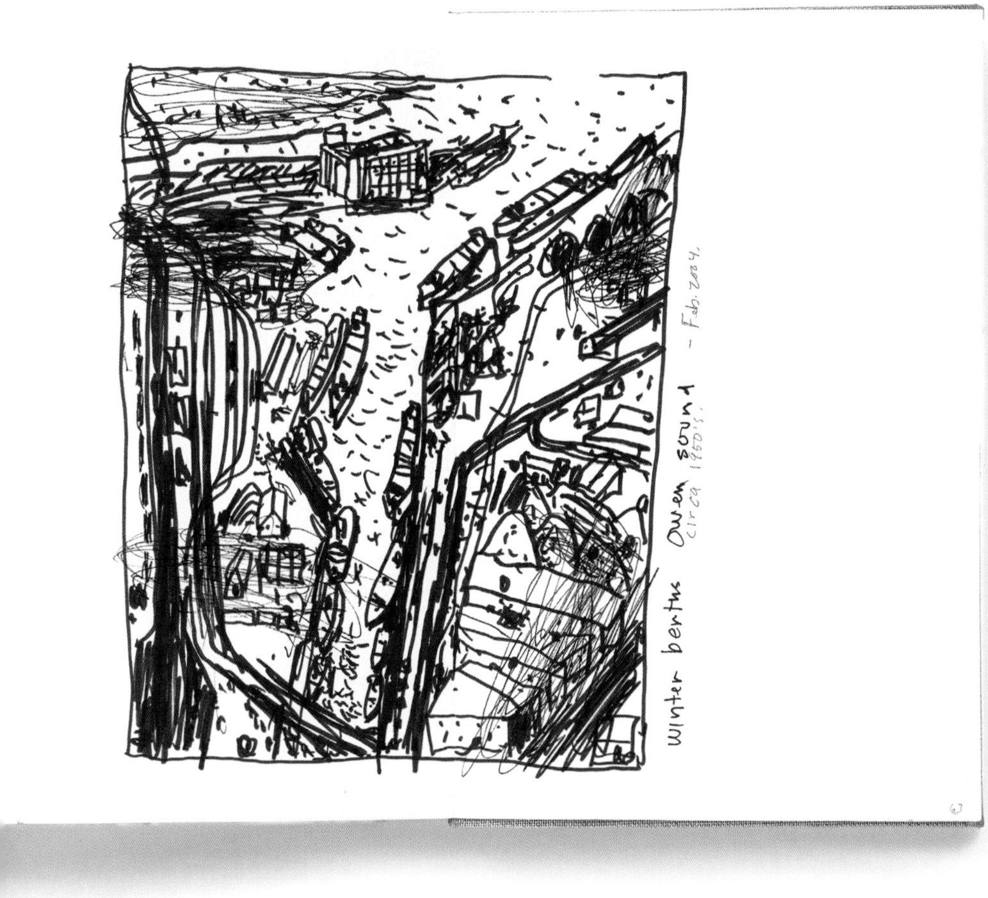
Winter berths Owen Sound
circa 1950s.
- Feb. 2004.

OWEN SOUND
2005
Oil on linen
168 x 152 cm (66 x 60 inches)

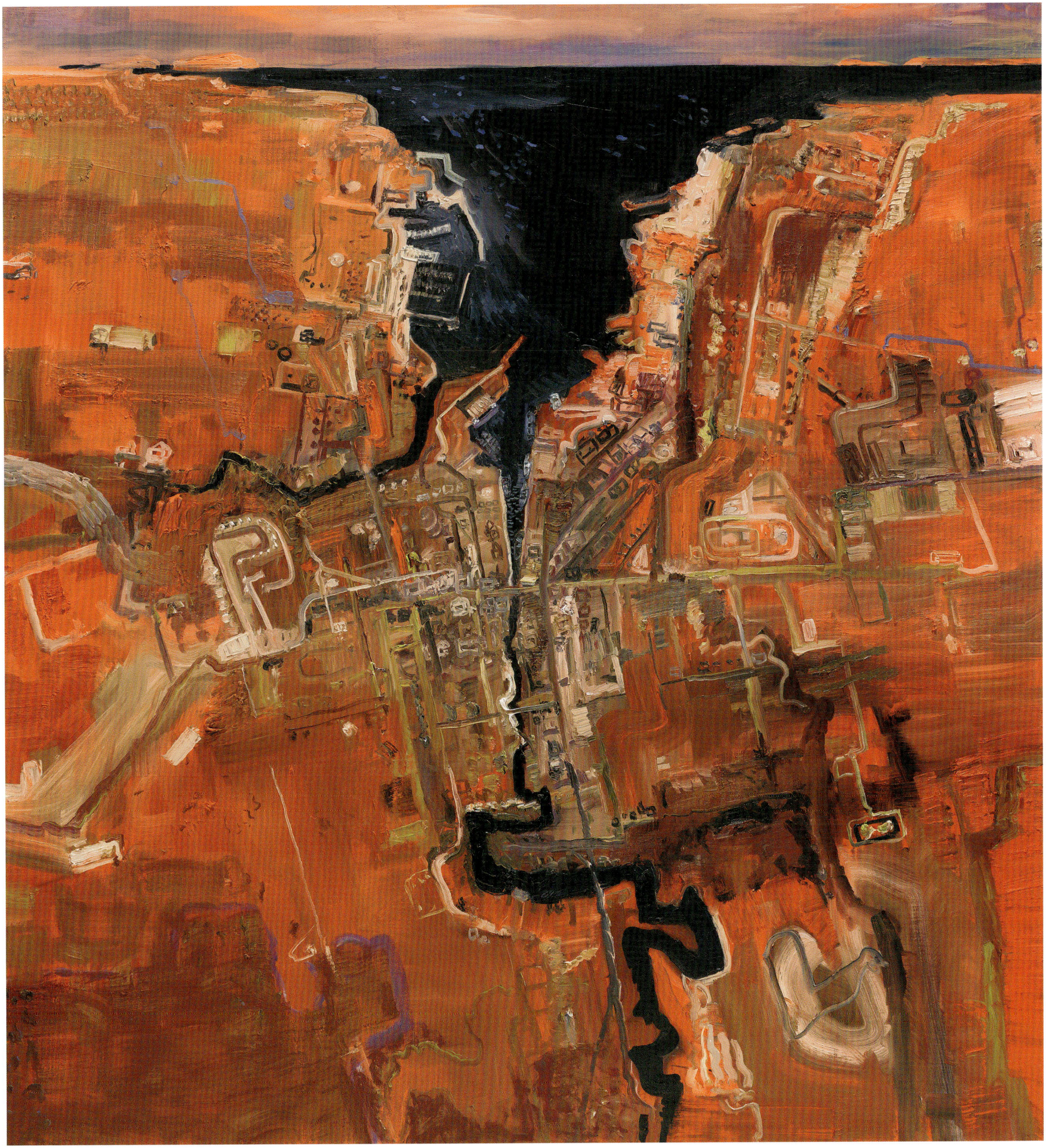

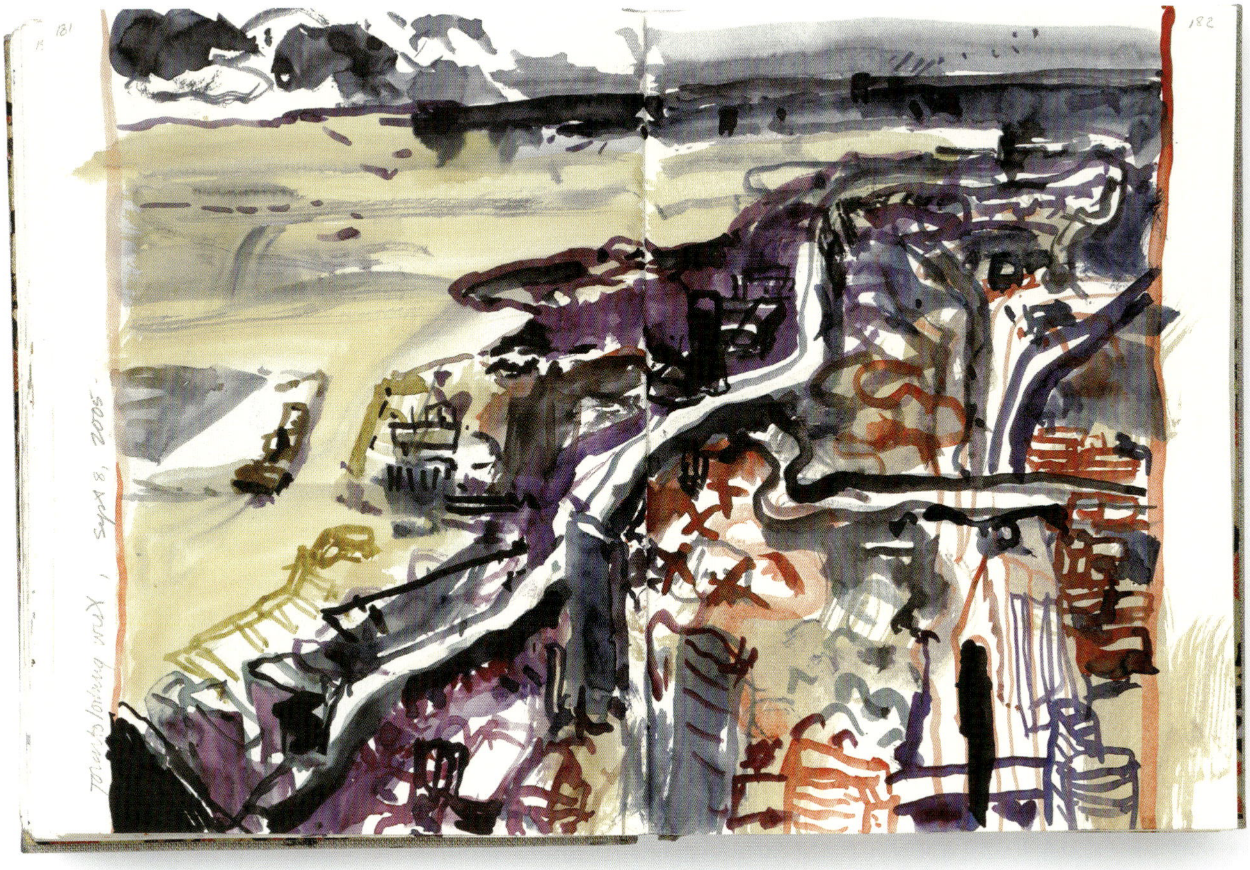

TORONTO LOOKING WEST

2005

Watercolour and graphite on paper; Coptic bound sketchbook 3, pp. 181–182, bound paper, 280 pages

22 x 17 cm (8.5 x 6.5 inches), folded

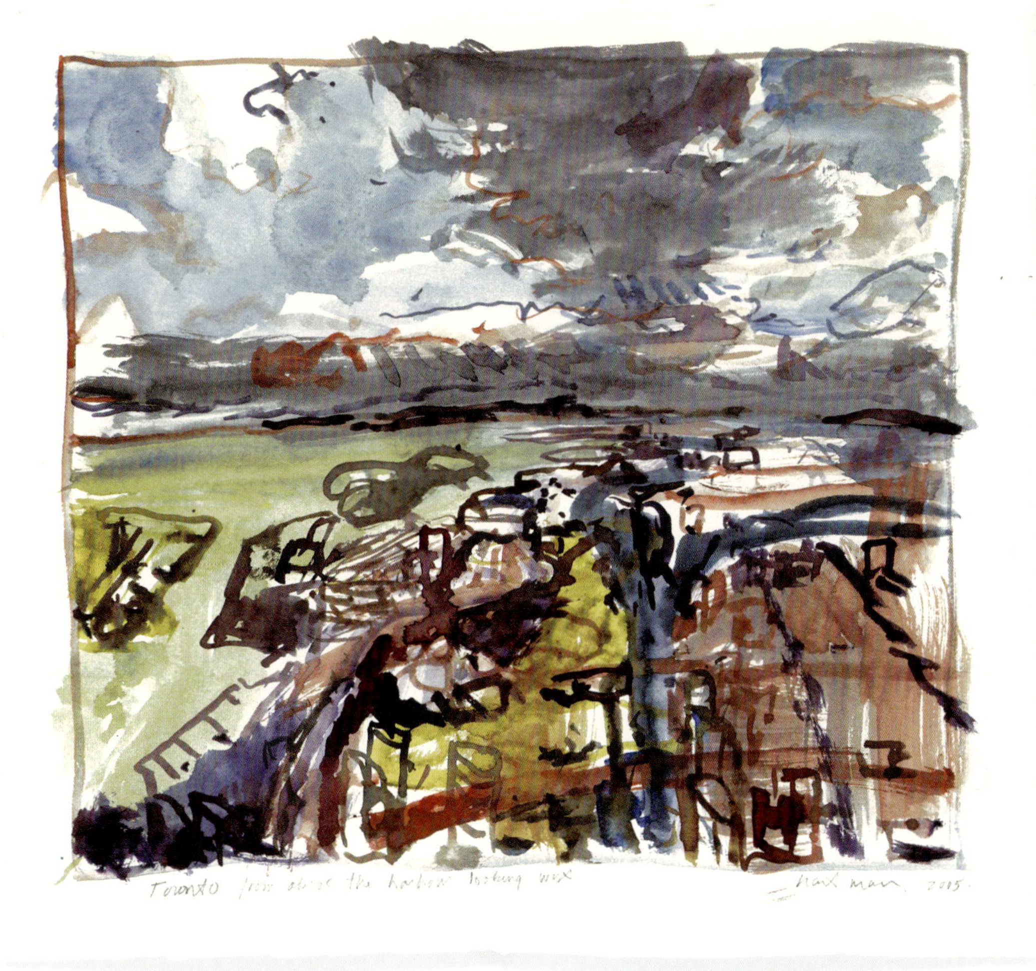

TORONTO FROM ABOVE THE HARBOUR LOOKING WEST
2005
Watercolour on paper
28.5 x 30 cm (11.25 x 12 inches)

THE WESTERN CHANNEL, TORONTO
2006
Oil on linen
152 x 168 cm (60 x 66 inches)

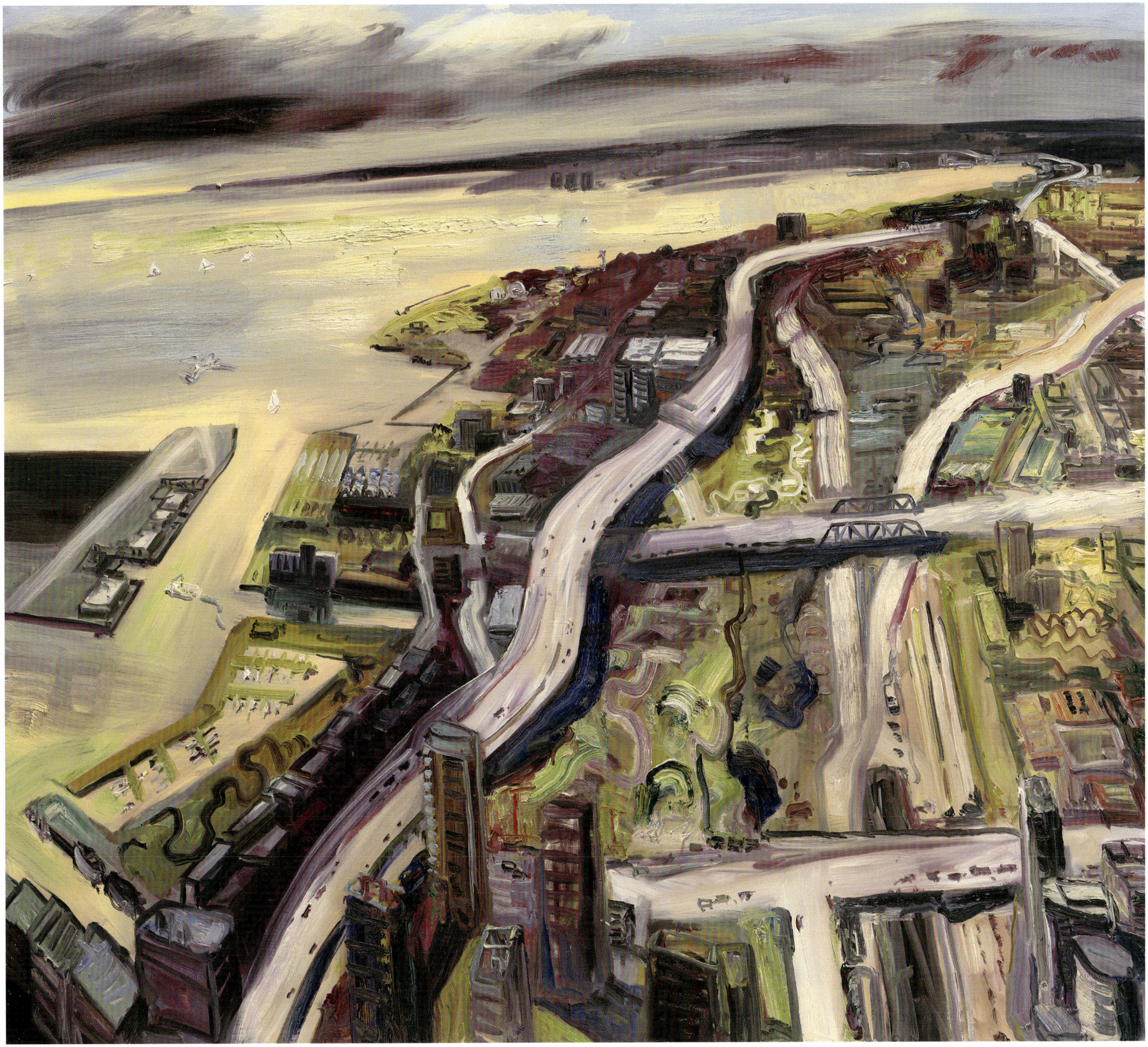

TORONTO HARBOUR LOOKING EAST
2005
Oil on linen
117 x 132 cm (46 x 52 inches)

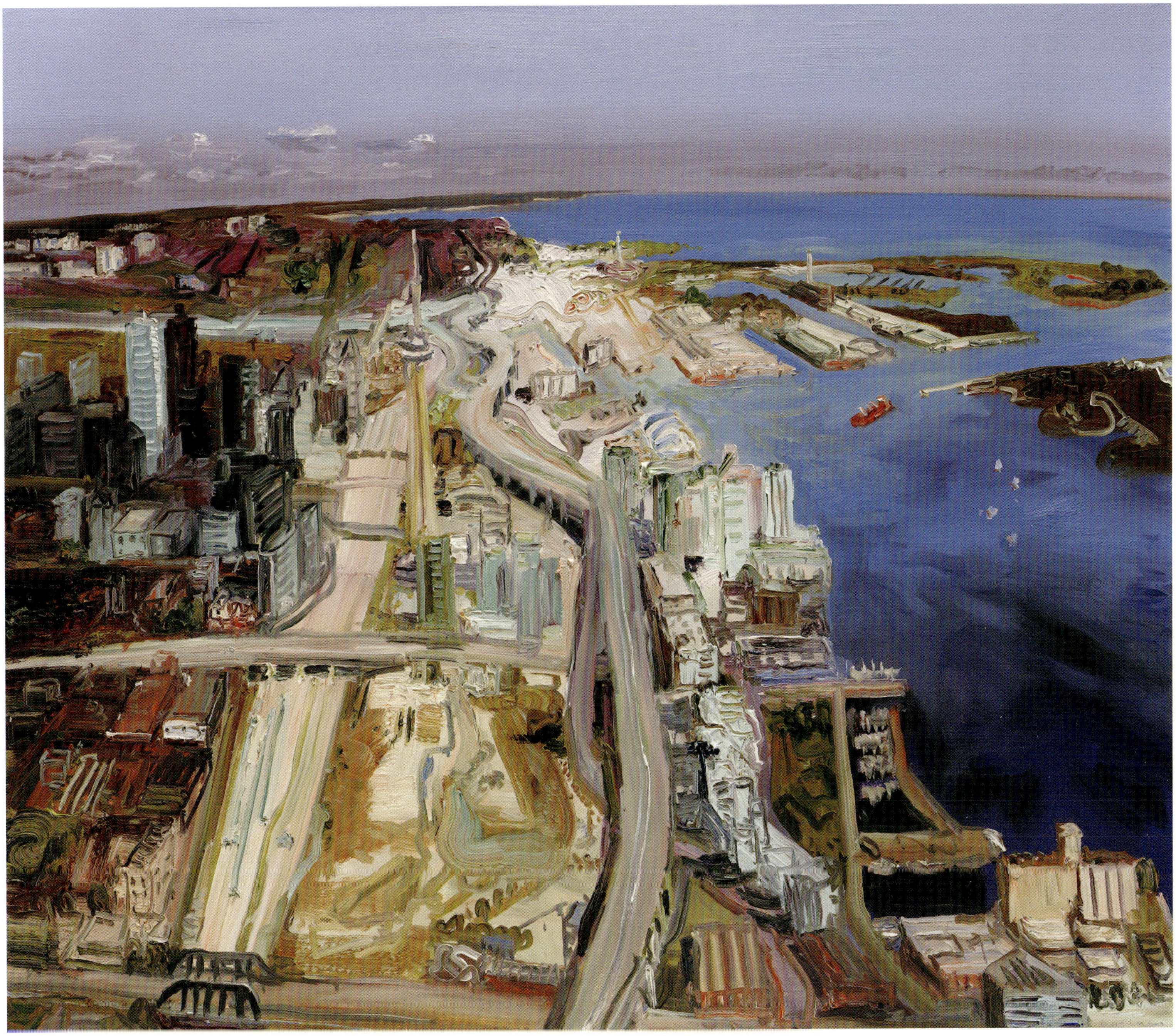

MONTREAL
2005
Oil on linen
122 x 137 cm (48 x 54 inches)

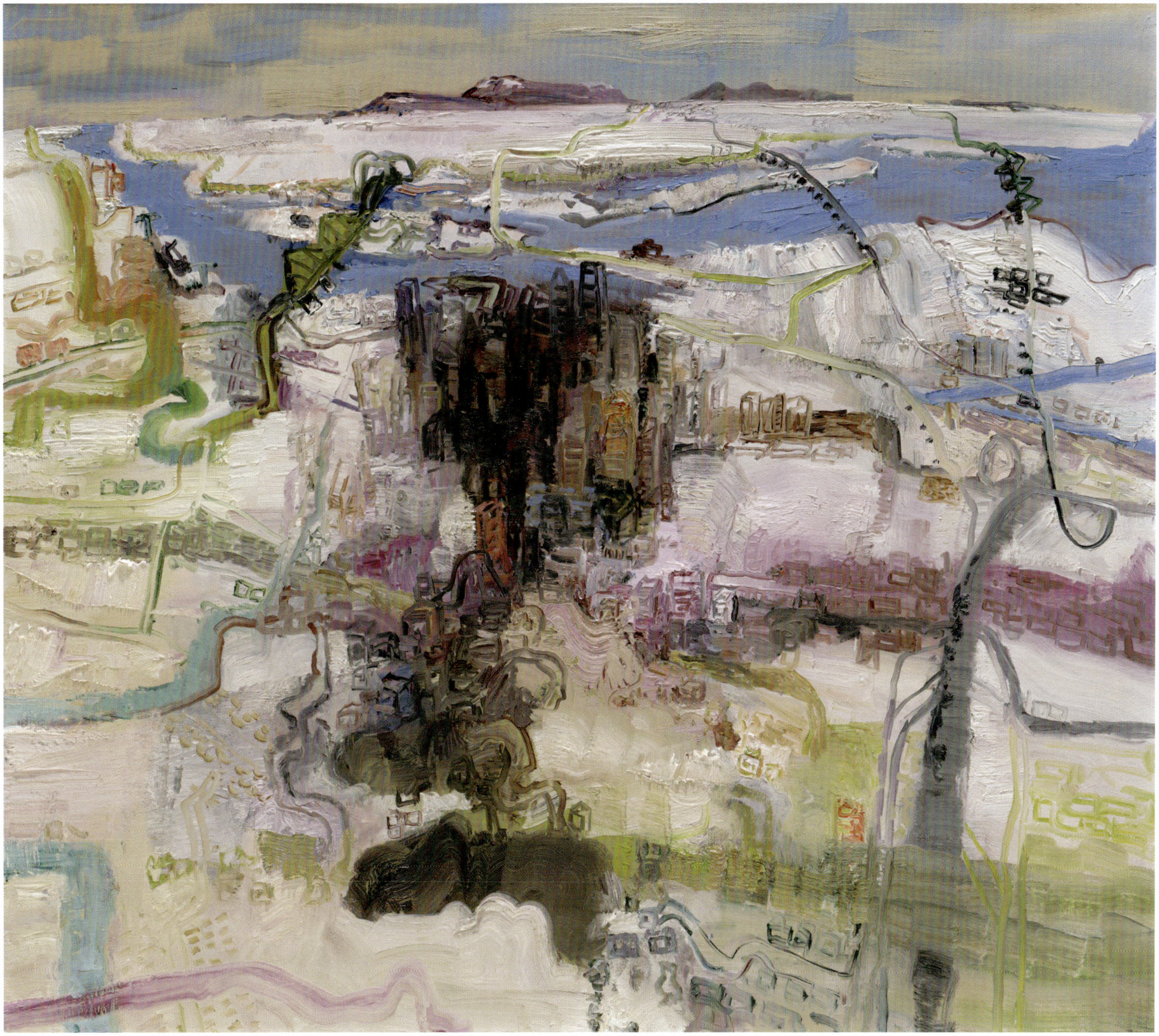

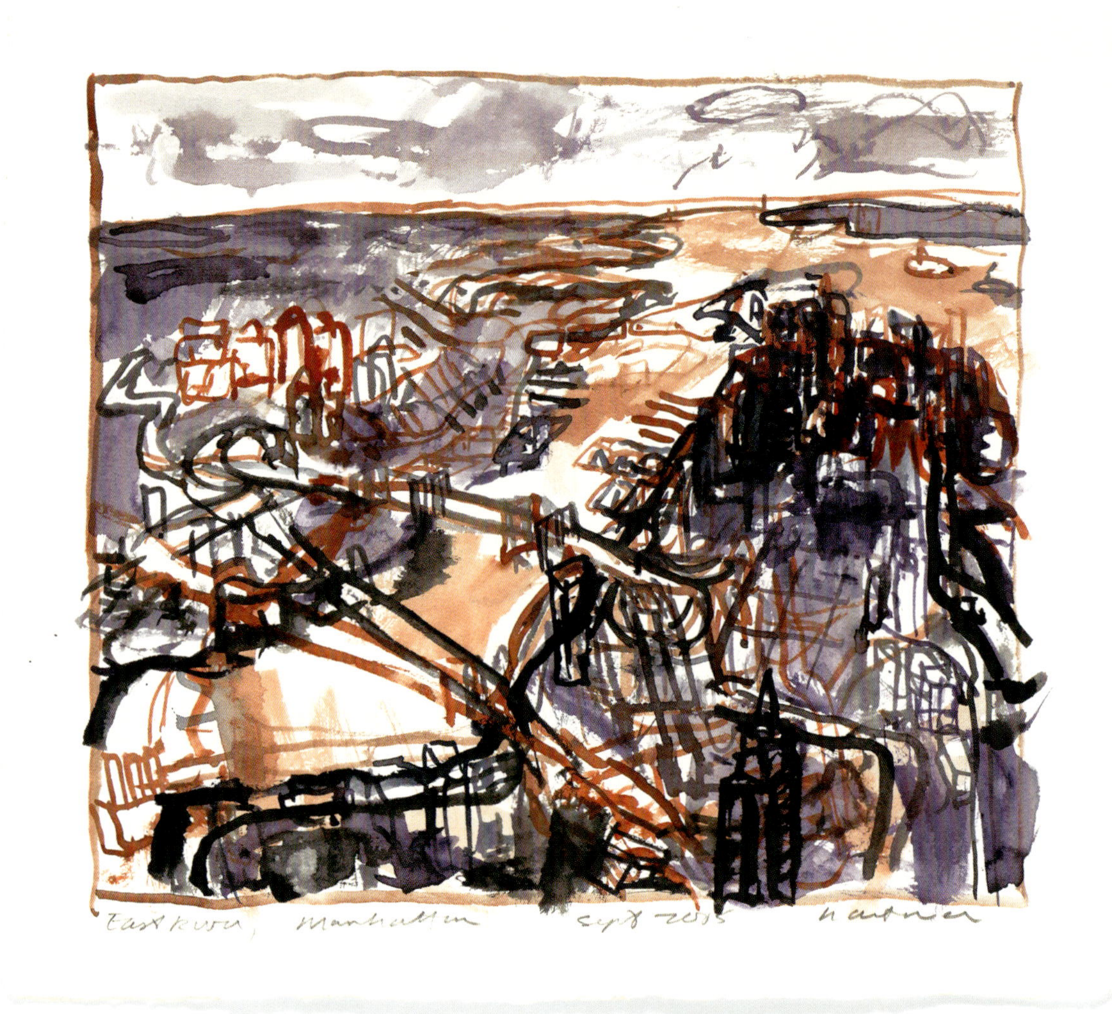

EAST RIVER, MANHATTAN
2005
Watercolour on paper
28.5 x 32 cm (11.25 x 12.5 inches)

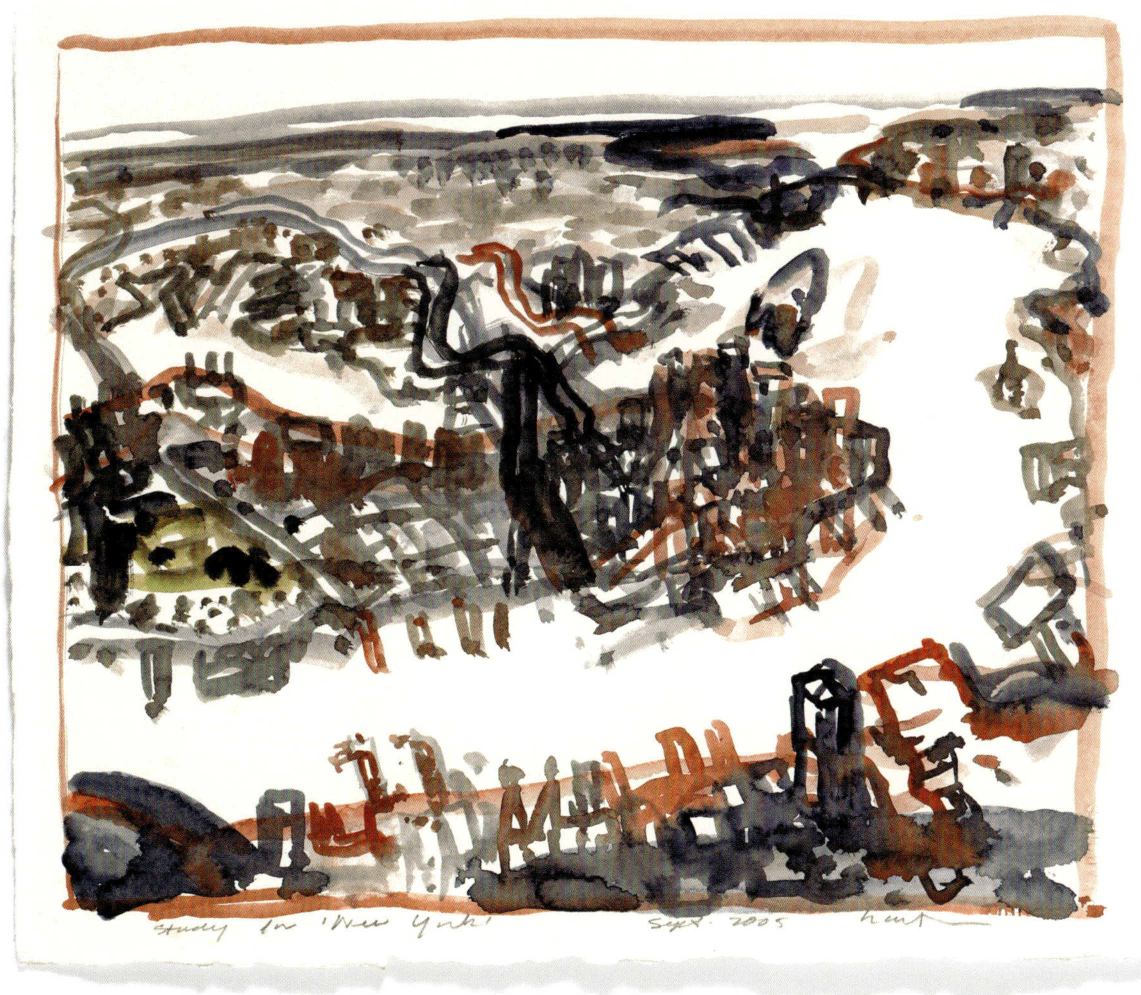

STUDY FOR NEW YORK
2005
Watercolour on paper
28.5 x 34 cm (11.25 x 13.25 inches)

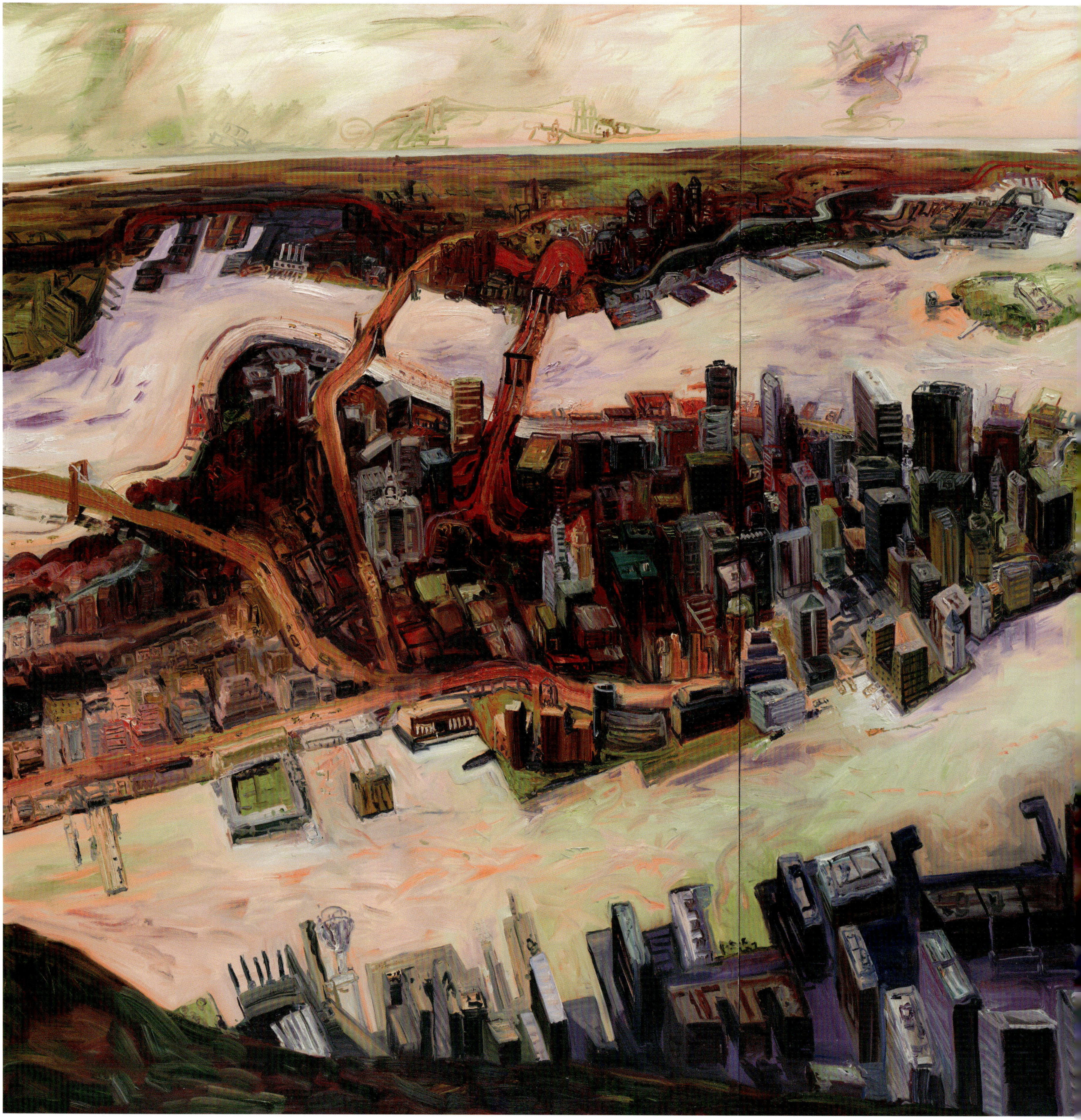

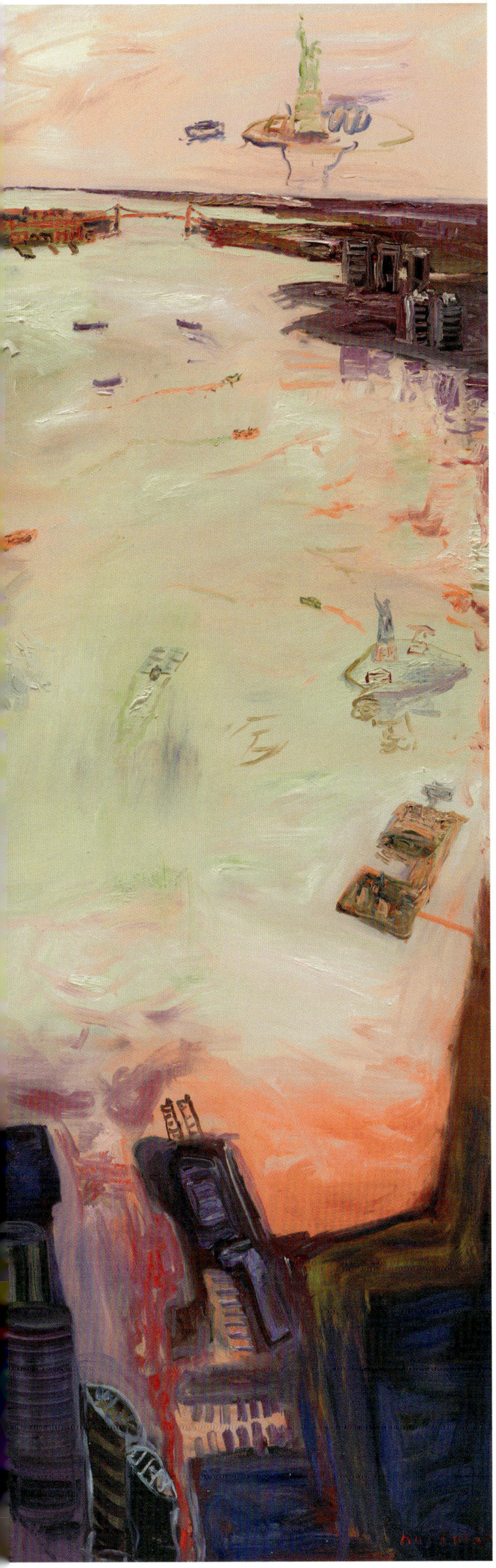

NEW YORK
2005
Oil on linen
251 x 335 cm (99 x 132 inches), diptych

MANHATTAN FROM ABOVE BROOKLYN

2005

Oil on linen

152 x 168 cm (60 x 66 inches)

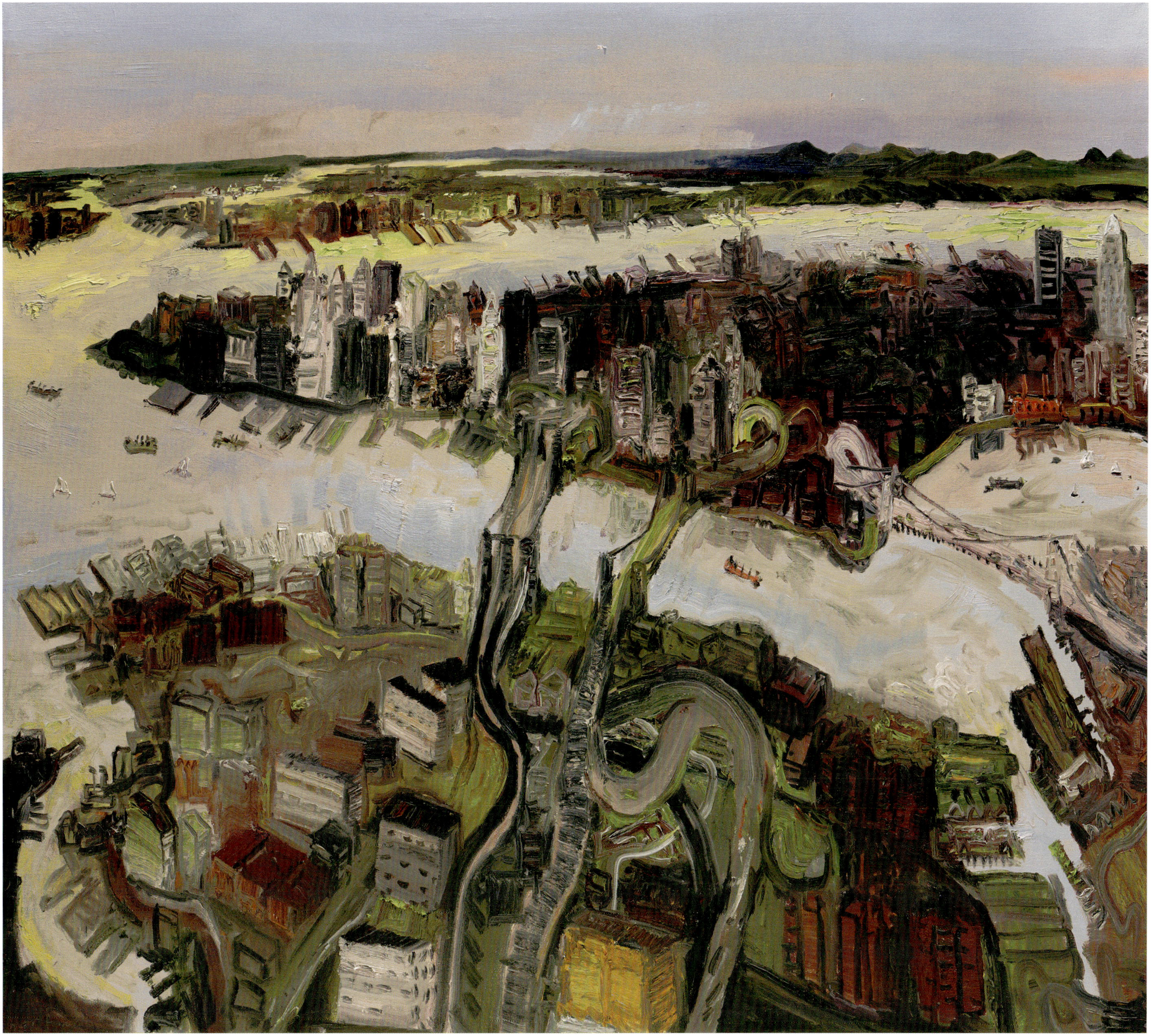

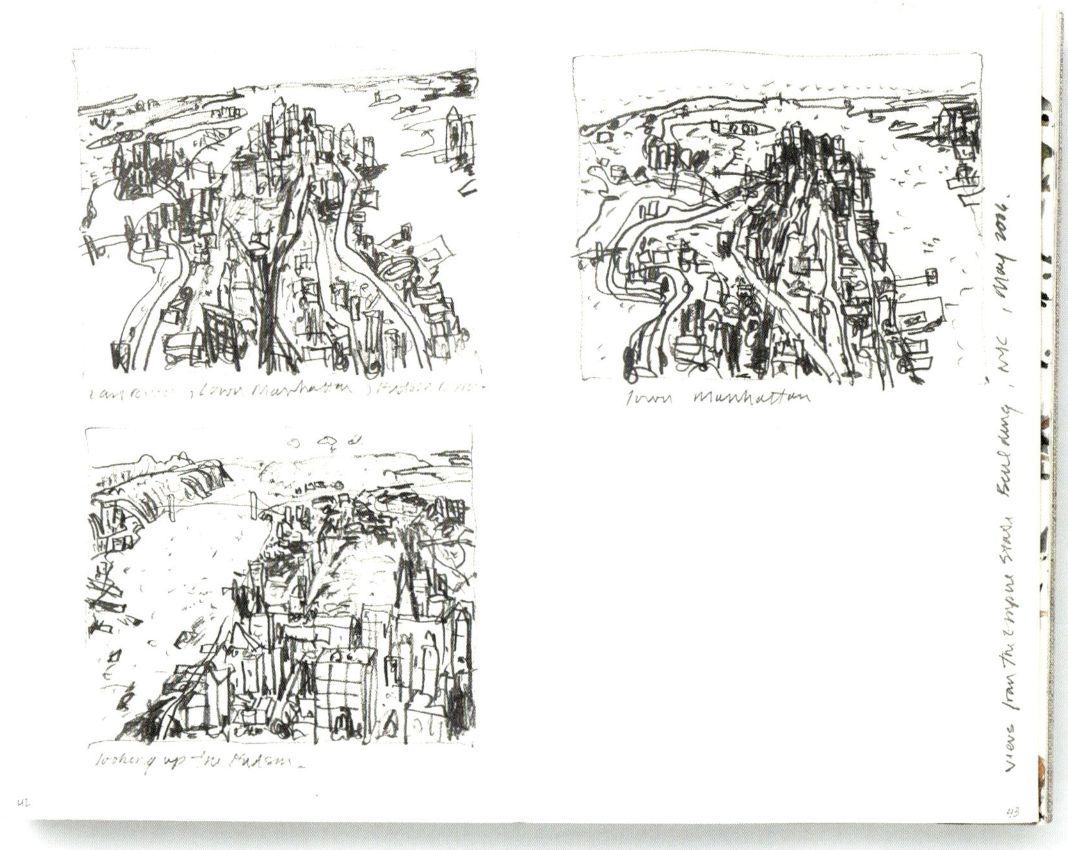

VIEWS FROM THE EMPIRE STATE BUILDING, NEW YORK CITY
2006
Graphite on paper; Concertina folding sketchbook 1, pp. 42–43, bound paper, 138 pages
24 x 17 cm (9.5 x 6.5 inches), folded

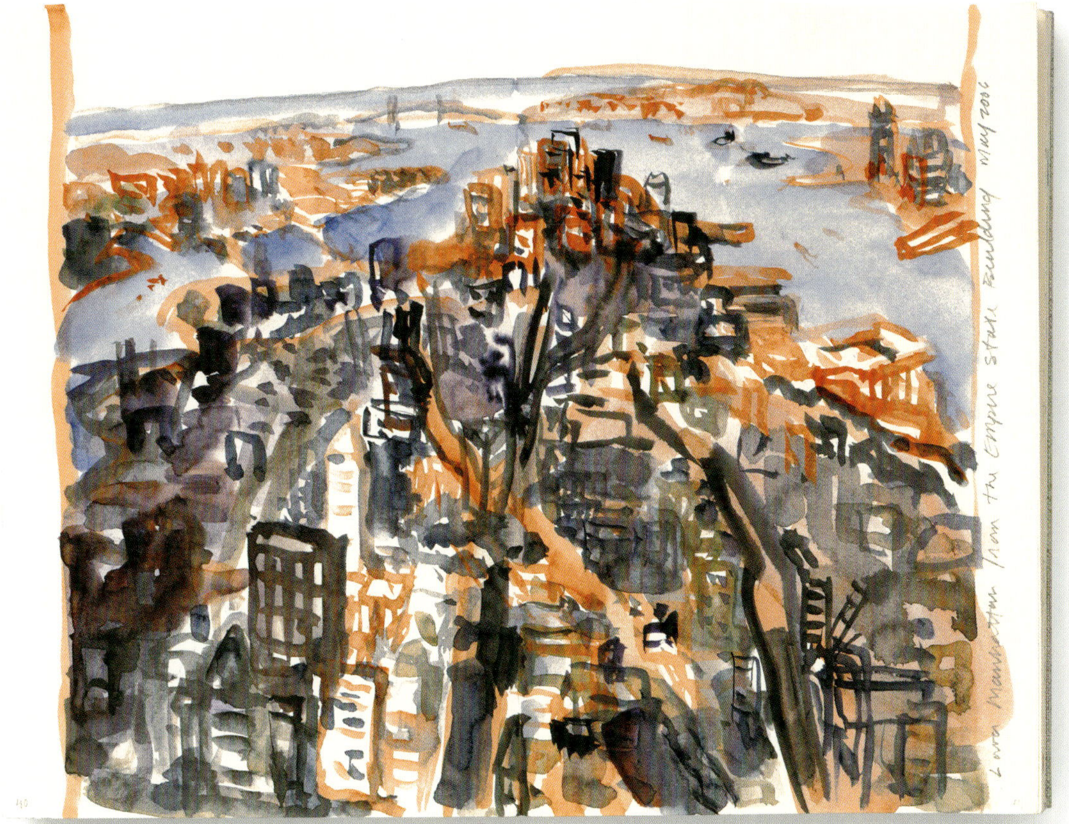

LOWER MANHATTAN FROM THE EMPIRE STATE BUILDING
2006
Watercolour and graphite on paper; Concertina folding sketchbook 1, pp. 40–41, bound paper, 138 pages
24 x 17 cm (9.5 x 6.5 inches), folded

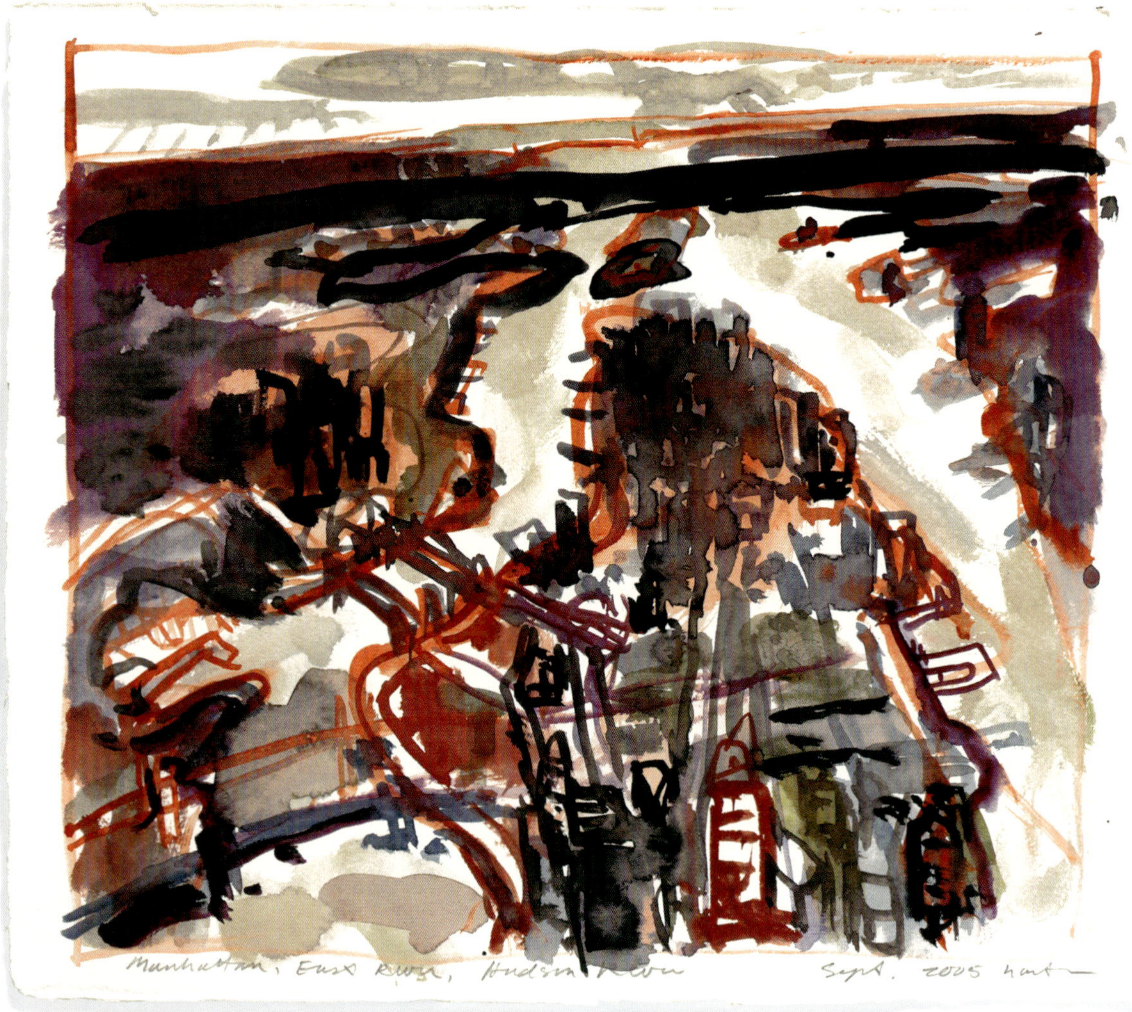

MANHATTAN, EAST RIVER, HUDSON RIVER
2005
Watercolour on paper
28.5 x 32 cm (11.25 x 12.5 inches)

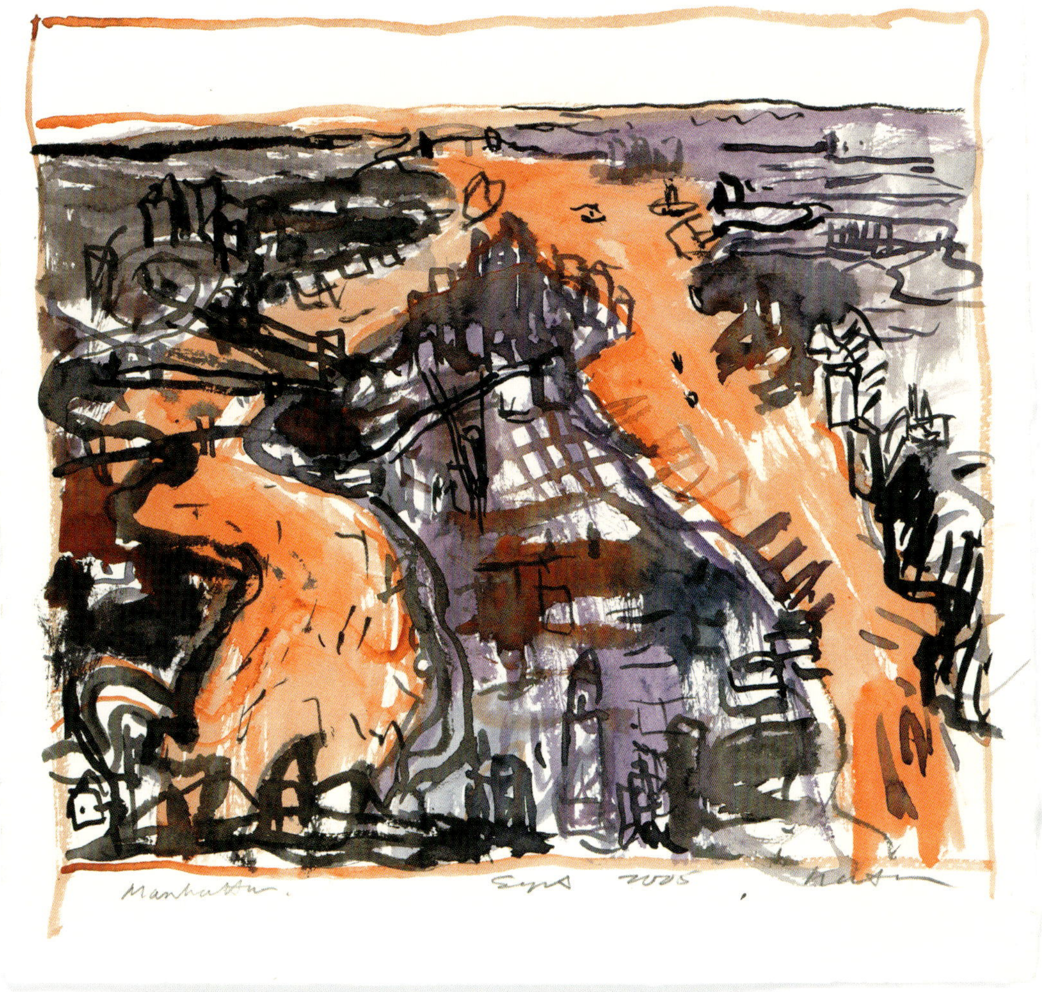

MANHATTAN
2005
Watercolour on paper
28.5 x 29 cm (11.25 x 11.5 inches)

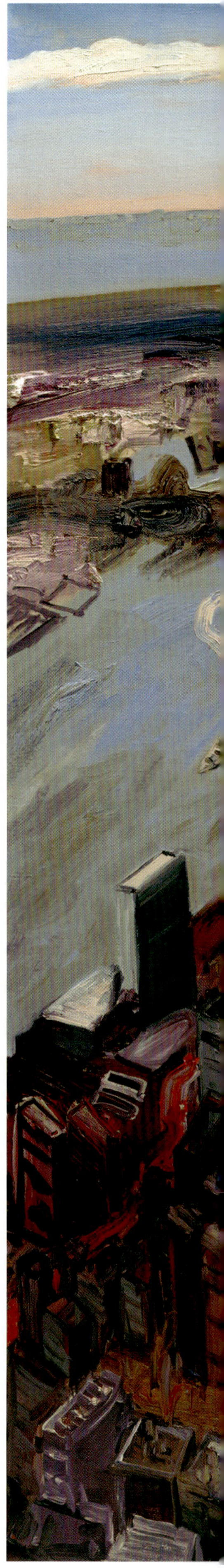

LOWER MANHATTAN
2006
Oil on linen
198 x 229 cm (78 x 90 inches)

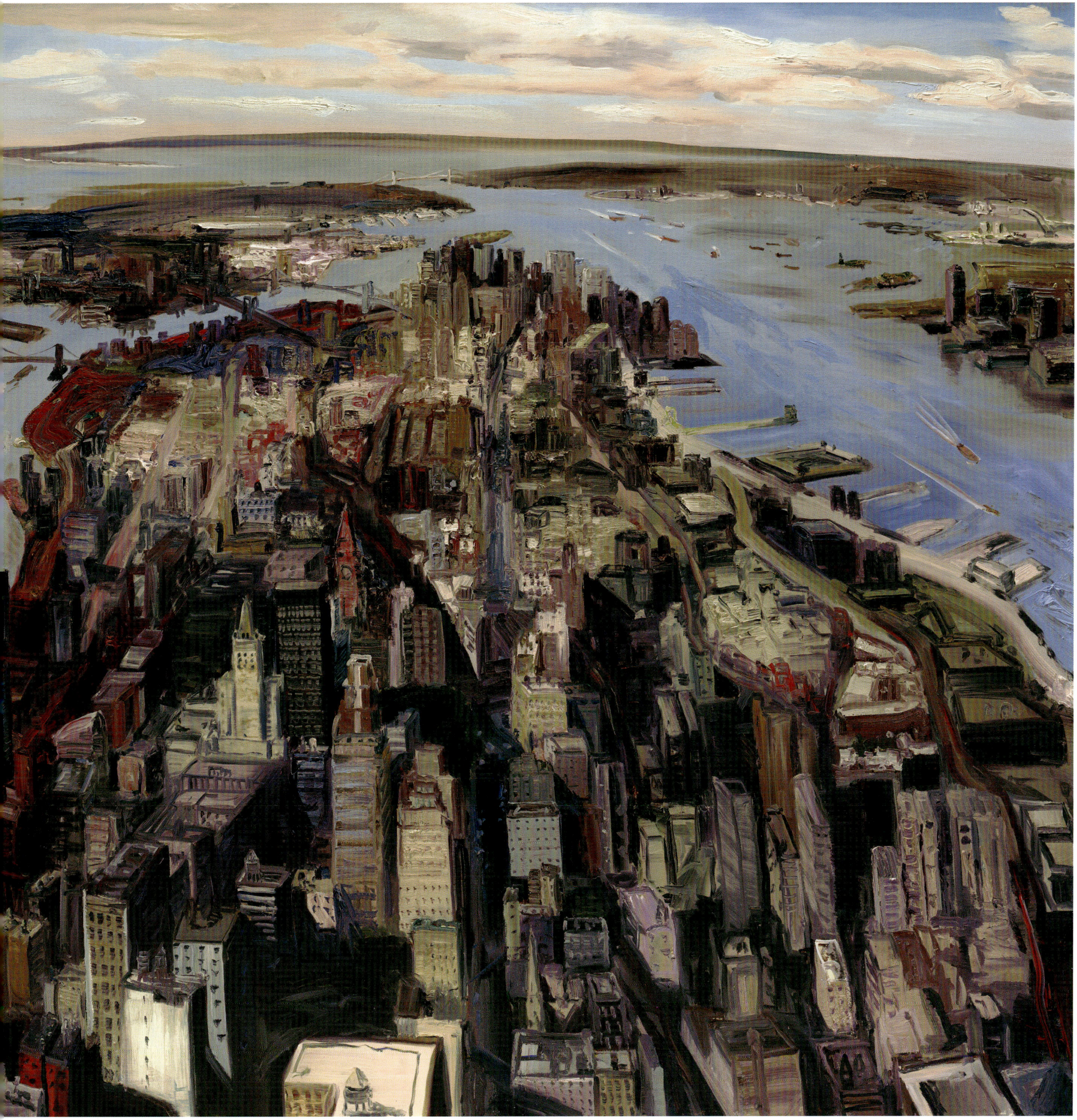

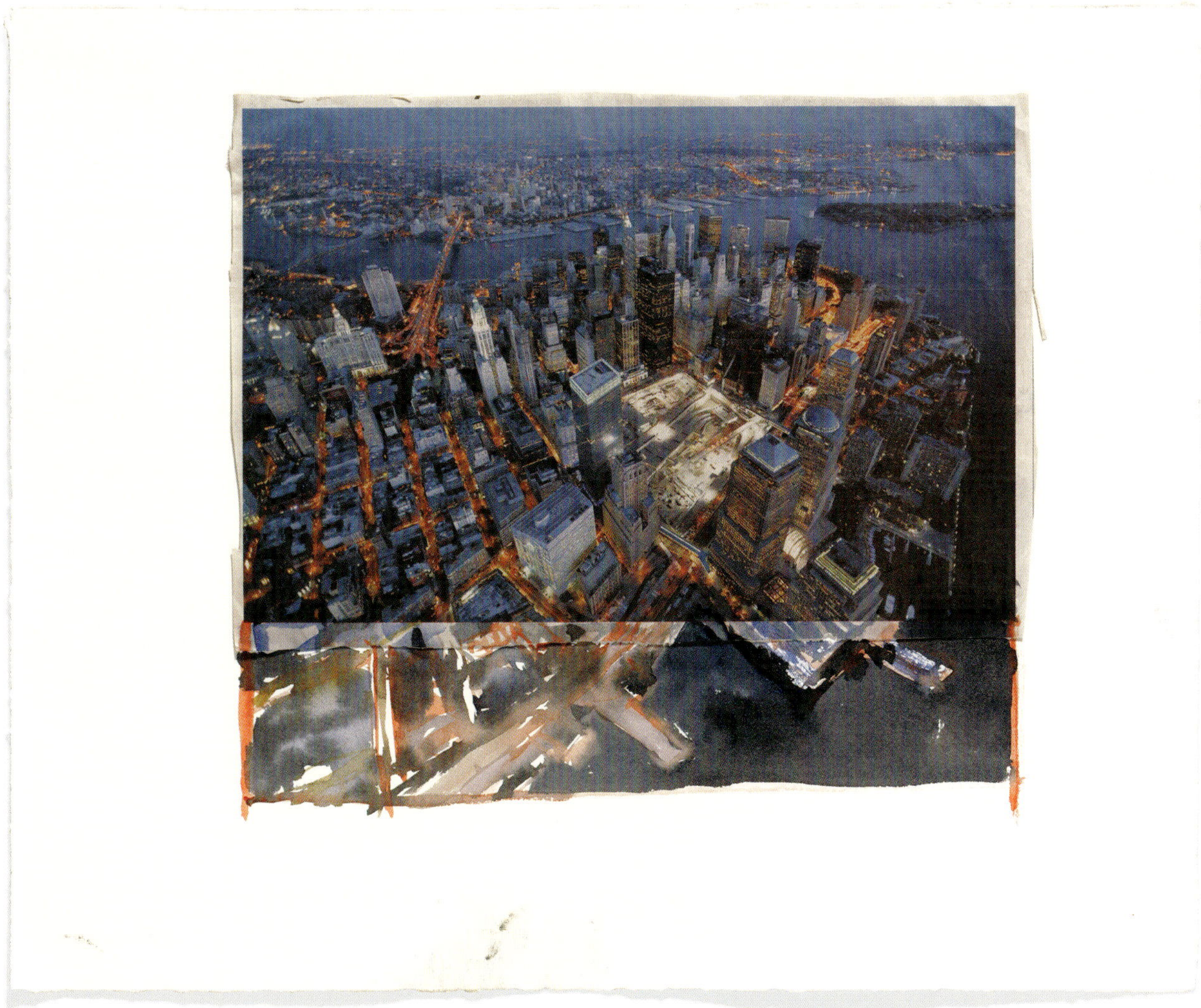

STUDY FOR MANHATTAN AT NIGHT
2006
Watercolour and newspaper illustration on paper
28.5 x 32 cm (11.25 x 12.5 inches)

MANHATTAN AT NIGHT
2006
Oil on linen
152 x 168 cm (60 x 66 inches)

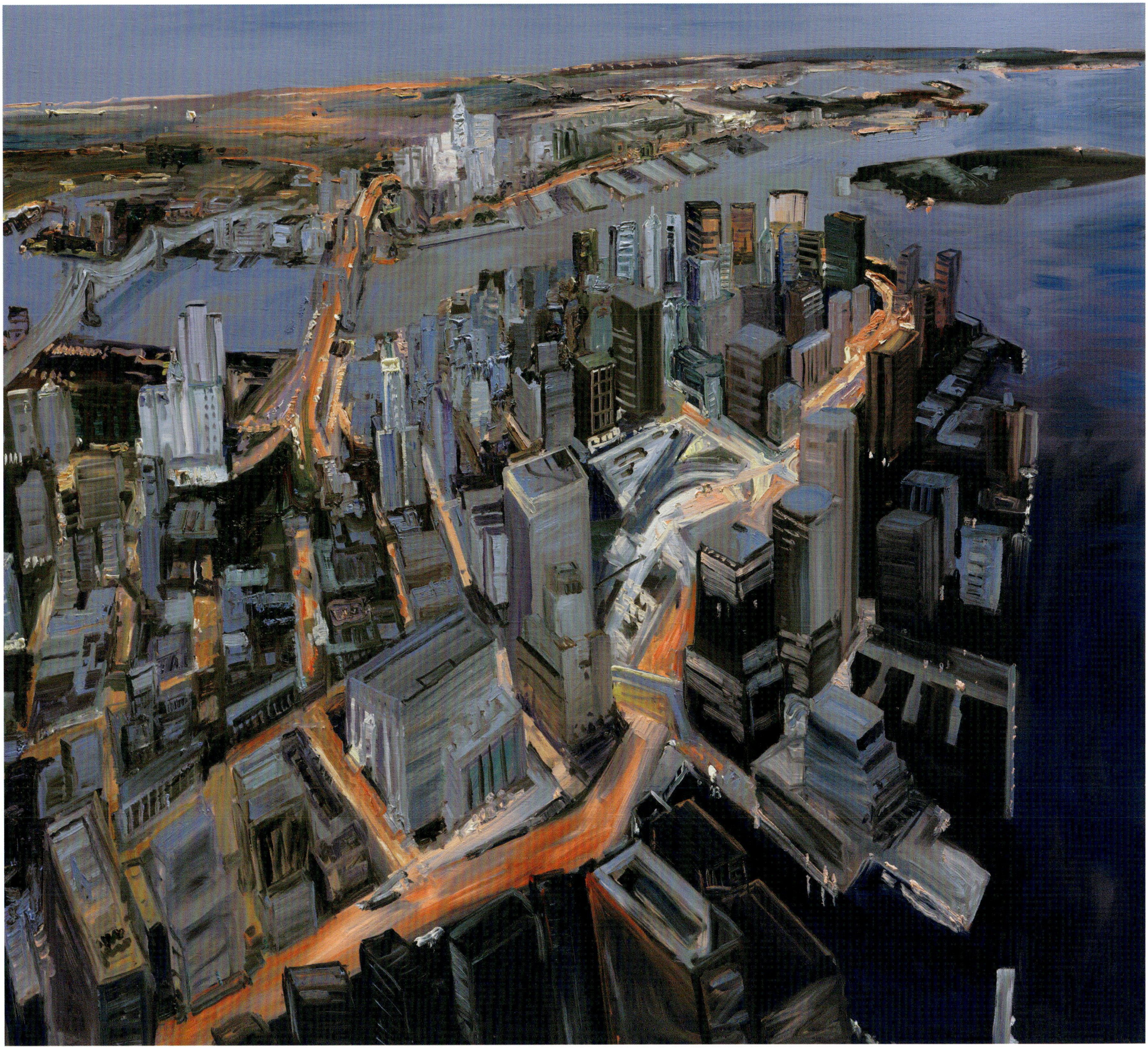

THE SOUTHSIDE HILLS, ST. JOHN'S
2004
Oil on linen
122 x 137 cm (48 x 54 inches)

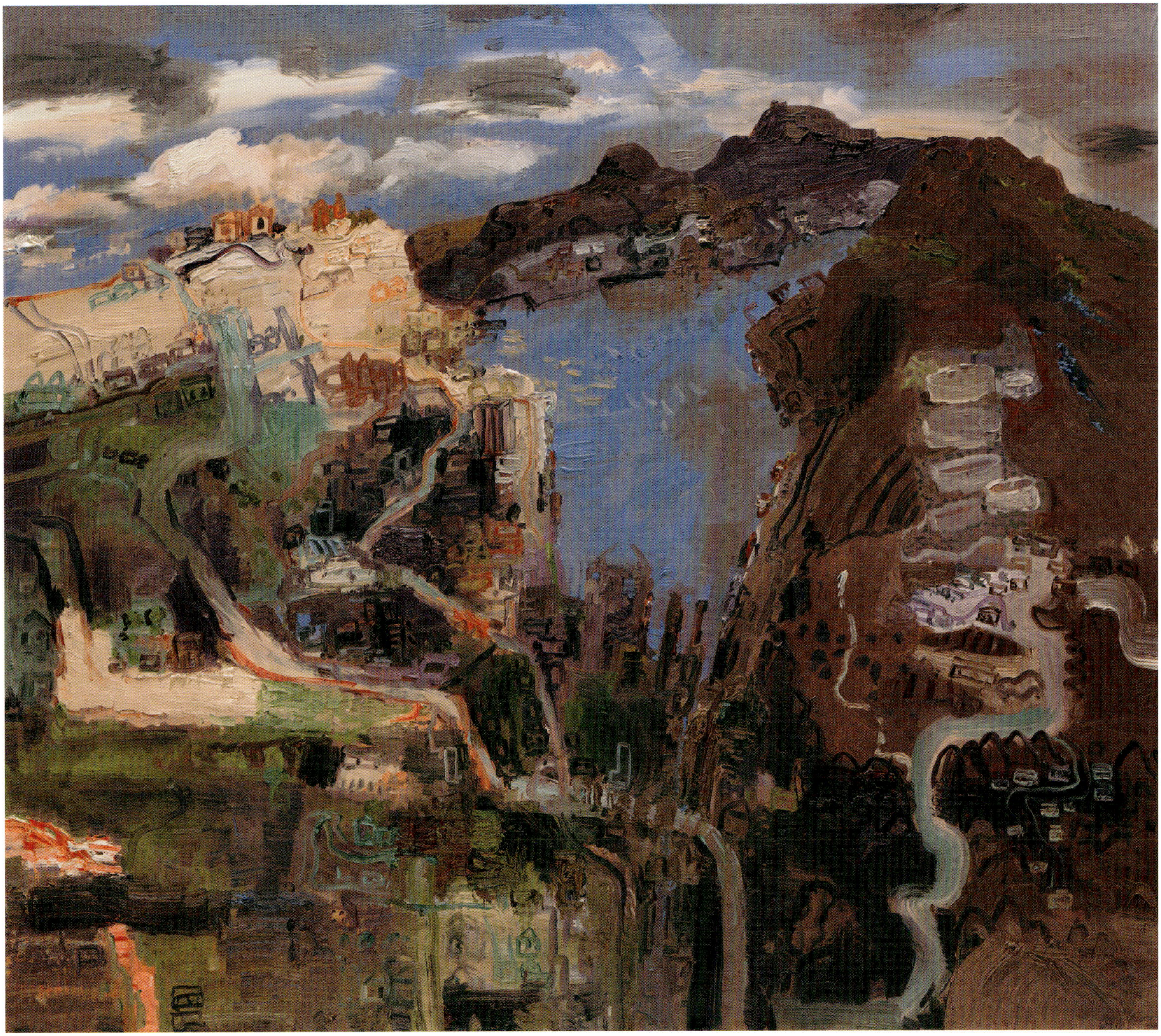

GLASGOW
2004
Oil on linen
122 x 137 cm (48 x 54 inches)

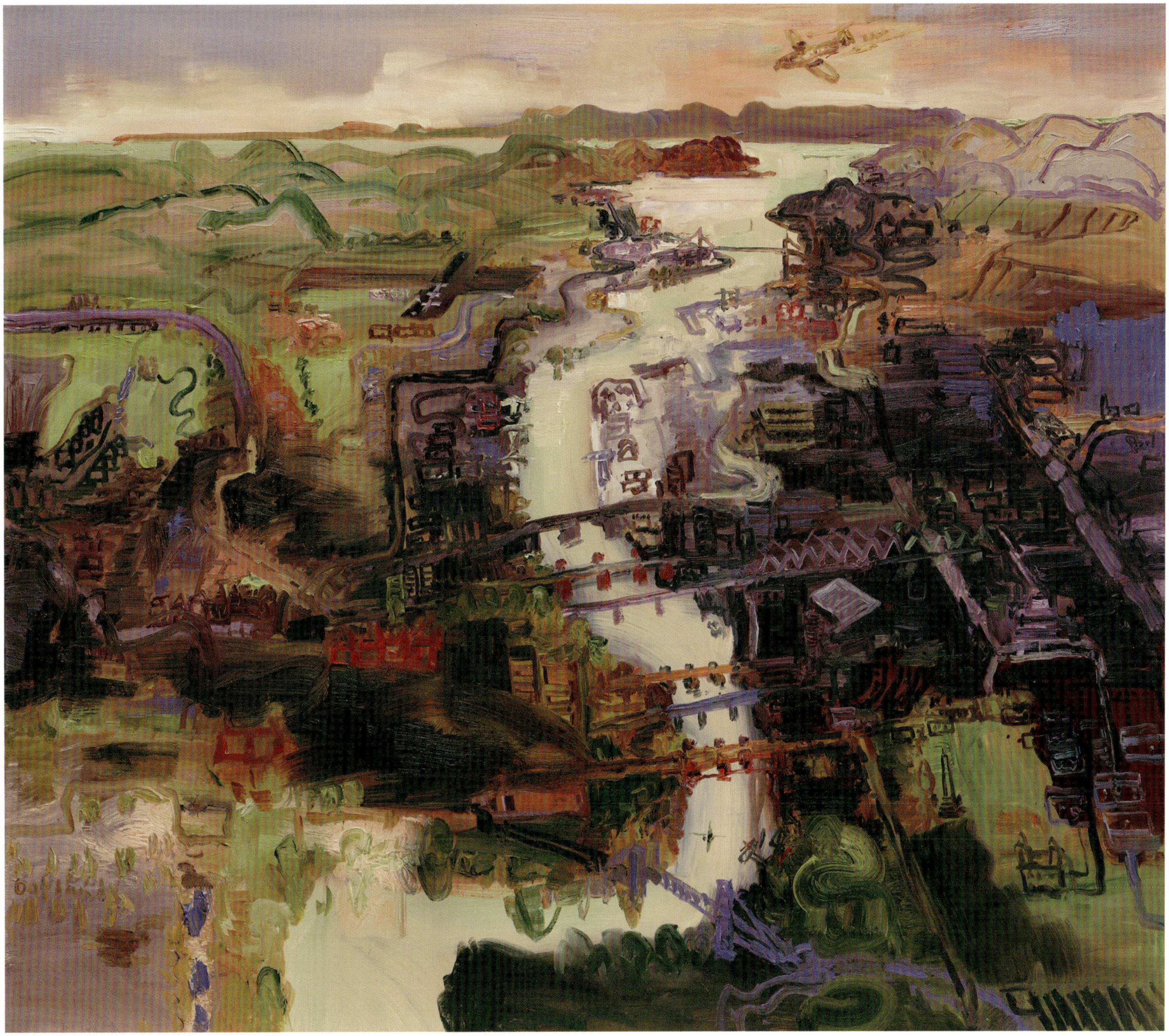

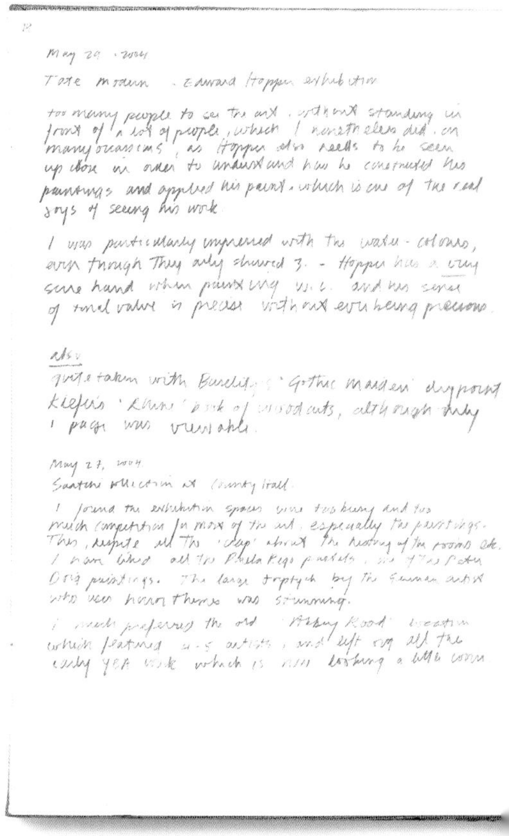

May 29 · 2004

Tate modern - Edward Hopper exhibition

too many people to see the art without standing in front of a lot of people, which I nonetheless did on many occasions, as Hopper also needs to be seen up close in order to understand how he constructed his paintings and applied his paint. which is one of the real joys of seeing his work

I was particularly impressed with the water-colours, even though they only showed 3. - Hopper has a very sure hand when painting w.c. and his sense of tonal value is precise without ever being precious.

also
quite taken with Burchfield's 'Gothic Maiden' drypoint
Kiefer's 'Rhine' book of woodcuts, although only 1 page was viewable.

May 27, 2004
Saatchi collection at County Hall.

I found the exhibition spaces were too busy and too much competition for most of the art, especially the paintings. Thus, despite all the 'crap' about the heating of the rooms etc. I [illegible] liked all the Paula Rego pastels, [illegible] Peter Doig paintings. The large triptych by the German artist who uses horror themes was stunning.

I much preferred the old 'Abbey Road' location which featured 4-5 artists, and left out all the early YBA work which is now looking a little [illegible]

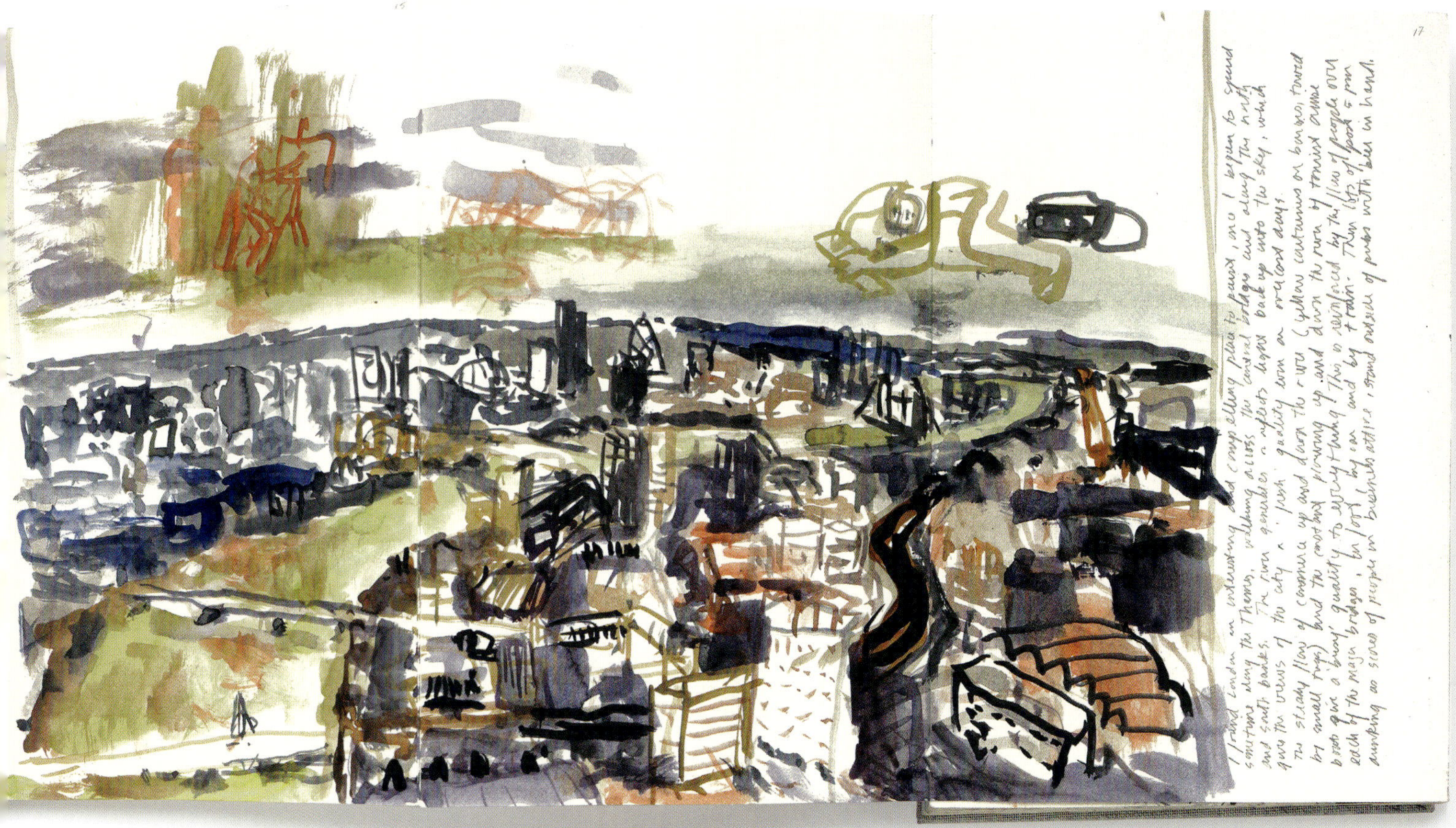

THE THAMES
2004
Watercolour and graphite on paper; Concertina folding sketchbook 2, pp. 14–17, bound paper, 138 pages
24 x 17 cm (9.5 x 6.5 inches), folded

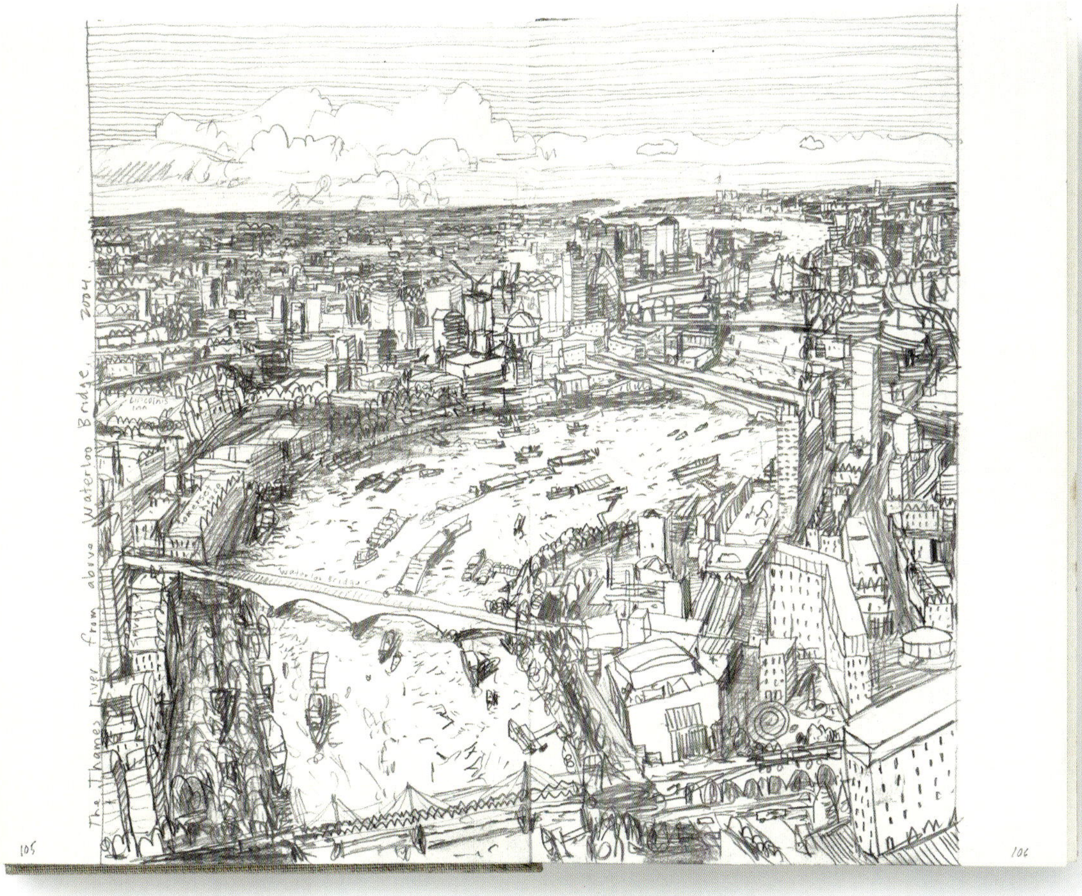

THE THAMES RIVER FROM ABOVE WATERLOO BRIDGE
2004
Pencil on paper; Concertina folding sketchbook 2, pp. 105–106, bound paper, 138 pages
24 x 17 cm (9.5 x 6.5 inches), folded

THE THAMES FROM SWISS RE
2005
Oil on linen
152 x 168 cm (60 x 66 inches)

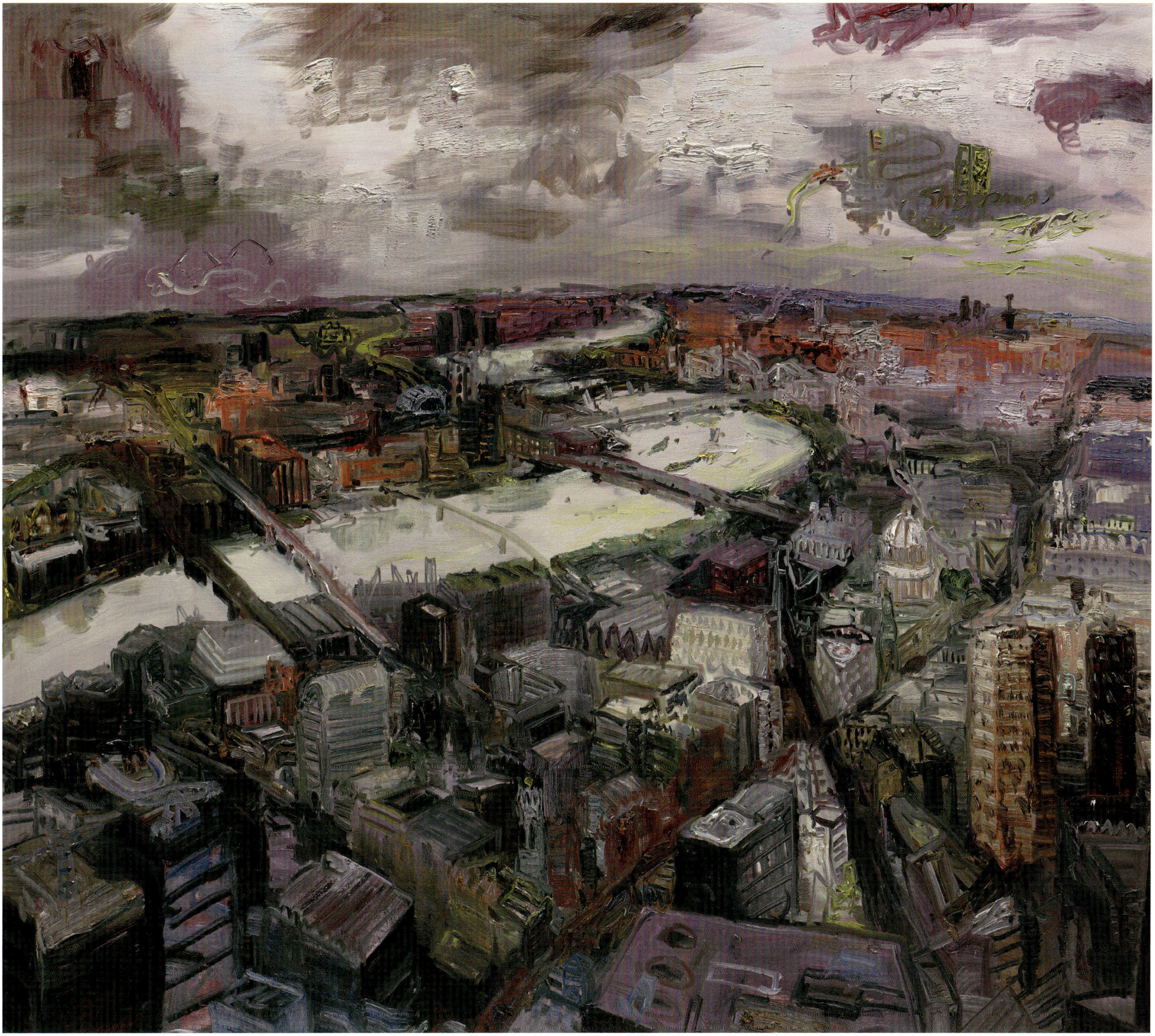

THE THAMES LOOKING WEST FROM ABOVE TOWER BRIDGE
2004
Oil on linen
122 x 137 cm (48 x 54 inches)

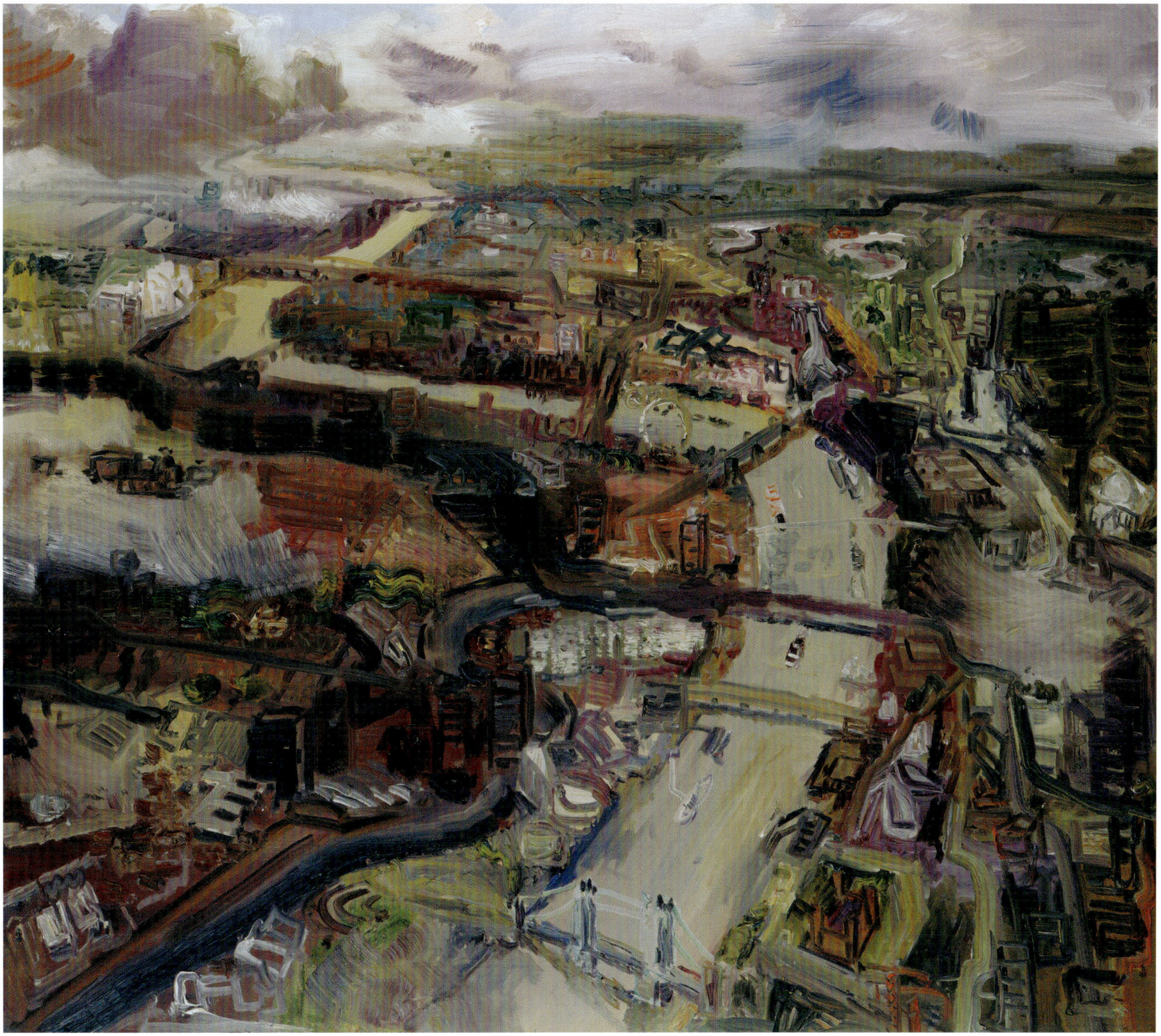

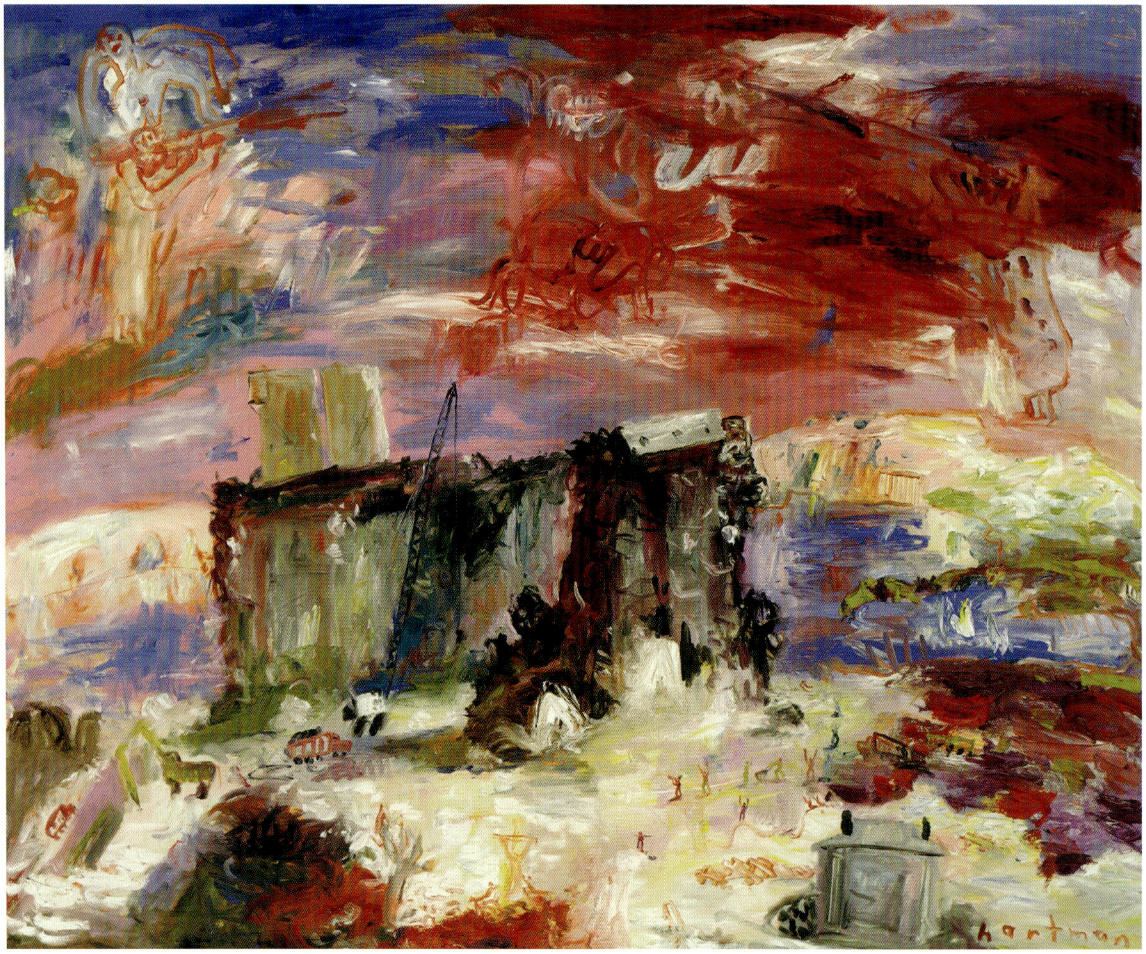

Fig. 1 John Hartman, *Jericho: Wrecking the Midland Simcoe*, 1992, oil on linen, 152 x 183 cm (60 x 72 inches). Tom Thomson Art Gallery, Owen Sound.

THE ECSTATIC CITY

STUART REID

During his well-documented painting career, John Hartman has consistently focused on landscapes that are familiar to him. His paintings have always included the varied evidence of the human footprint. For Hartman, it is false to portray the landscape as a pristine wilderness. Evidence of highways, people, towns, vehicles, and industry is always present. He acknowledges that human life cannot be separated from nature, and that our impact on the world can be both good and bad, but cannot be ignored.

In 1981, Hartman established a studio near Midland in Lafontaine, Ontario. Having grown up there and then chosen to resettle there as an adult, Hartman has a unique claim on the landscapes and landmarks of the Georgian Bay area. He has developed a rich relationship with those landscapes, conducting extensive research into the local history, both recent and distant, of the towns and settlements of the bay's southern shores. His intimate familiarity with the place has allowed him to create a kind of figurative shorthand that he uses to relay the stories of people—his paintings of the last two decades often contain pictographs, ghostly renderings of characters or events that are roughly sketched in the paint. It is as if the artist has a supernatural ability to see the shimmering visual residue of lives lived—momentous events as apparitions hung in the sky, high above the land.

Hartman's paintings acknowledge the deep spiritual connection that exists between the landscape and the people who live on it. The painting *Jericho: Wrecking the Midland Simcoe* (fig. 1) gives an event in a small Ontario town the gravity of an Old Testament story. The wrecking of the grain elevator in Midland Harbour marked the eradication of a local landmark—Hartman links that destruction with the story of the city of Jericho, which was destroyed and rebuilt several times over several hundred years. The equation of a small-town event with ancient history—the local with the mythic—is a recurring device in Hartman's painting. By rooting his work in the familiar, he forefronts the individual's perspective. In so doing, he pinpoints the quiet futility one often feels in the face of time and the ongoing march of change: herein lies a poignancy that colours much of his work.

In the years since Hartman's re-establishment in Lafontaine, travels have taken him far from Georgian Bay. The places the artist is drawn to are often areas whose northern maritime culture reminds him of home: Newfoundland, England, Scotland, Denmark. In the paintings that document his travels, Hartman attempts to tap into the energy of the events that have transpired in a given location, the narratives that link people to place. Of course, history refers to the past and to that which is lost: loss seems to be the emotional anchor in many of Hartman's paintings. The artist shows us that the landscape and the cultural trappings embedded in it may appear to be permanent, but in fact are always changing. Concepts of home may root our psyches in a particular place, but our sense of connection and belonging to a place is sometimes only a comforting illusion. Investigating that longing to belong seems intrinsic to all of Hartman's work, including his more recent paintings of cities.

A series of paintings of Copenhagen, Denmark, from 1997 heralds Hartman's growing interest in cityscapes and his predilection for a high viewpoint. In 1981, Hartman began to paint the land from an aerial perspective that allowed him to push the horizon back far enough to show the curve of the Earth, suggesting deep space.[1] *KobenHavn—Western Approach* (fig. 2) contains such an aerial view and shows the artist's interest in the shape of the city's buildings and the mysterious dark water that cuts through the urban mesh. The vista stretches out to encompass the surrounding landscape and the sea. Hartman gives his cityscapes a particular tilt, an off-kilter skew that suggests the view from the window of a plane as it banks for an approach.

Hartman has said that "the transition to painting cities came very effortlessly and naturally to me because I see them in the same way [as landscapes]. I see them as a place; it's just that there is much more density and human activity there than there is in the outer islands of Georgian Bay."[2] Hartman has often painted the harbour cities that surround the bay: Port Severn, Parry Sound, and Owen Sound. In these paintings, the towns' low-density development clings tentatively to the edges of the water, punctuating the broad expanse of the landscape. Bridges are like lifelines tossed across the bay, linking small pockets of gridded streets amid the dramatic surrounding terrain. *Owen Sound* (p. 79), for example, makes apparent the city's history as an important Great Lakes port in the striking way that the dark, ominous waters of Georgian Bay infiltrate the landscape. The Sydenham River winds down from the open sound at the top of the painting to its bottom edge, cleaving the land mass into two halves. These paintings set the stage for Hartman's next subjects: cities like New York, London, Glasgow, Halifax, Toronto, Vancouver, and Hamilton, with all their urban complexity and their myriad lives and narratives.

The essence of a city is partly its legend, of course. Just the words "New York" conjure all sorts of impulses and emotions for those who have first-hand knowledge of the city, and even for those who don't. Contemplating New York conjures an adrenaline rush. Hartman's response is to bring the vibrant colours and sensual application of paint so commonly associated with landscape painting into his engagement with urban centres both small and large: florid colours applied with a juicy, overloaded brush in broad lyrical strokes characterize all of Hartman's city renderings. In *Lower Manhattan* (pp. 100–101) the spires of high-rises and office towers have the gaudy beauty of tall lupines in a summer garden. The painting depicts the urban core as a visceral, heaving mass of line, colour, and form, pulsing with burgeoning life. Portrayed in its sprawling wholeness, the city is a constantly evolving organism that weighs heavily on the natural landscape that surrounds it. One remembers the pace, the movement, the density—the city is too large, too busy for one to take it all in, and we must forsake awareness of the whole to focus on the immediate. In New York, an individual is but one insignificant part of the greater life force coursing through the streets. Correspondingly, the painting evokes the sensation of being consumed by stimulation.

Hartman's conceptual strategy in these paintings is to combine individual memory and collective history into a new vision of cities. Each city becomes a collective dreamscape, a universal, externalized understanding that is informed by many factors: memory, history, politics, film, literature, technology, and the media. What results is a multi-faceted view that straddles the realms of public and private but is larger than either of them—mythic, like Hartman's vision of the altered Midland Harbour.

When generating source imagery for his painting process, Hartman works from a point of immersion in his subject. He seeks to intimately know each city that he paints and searches for vantage points that will allow him to experience the skyline, to understand the mass of the metropolis, its shapes and colours, its natural contours and man-made constructions. He observes and absorbs his subject at street level, from airplanes, and from atop

[1] Ness, *with minimal means*, 4.

[2] John Hartman, interview with author, June 2006.

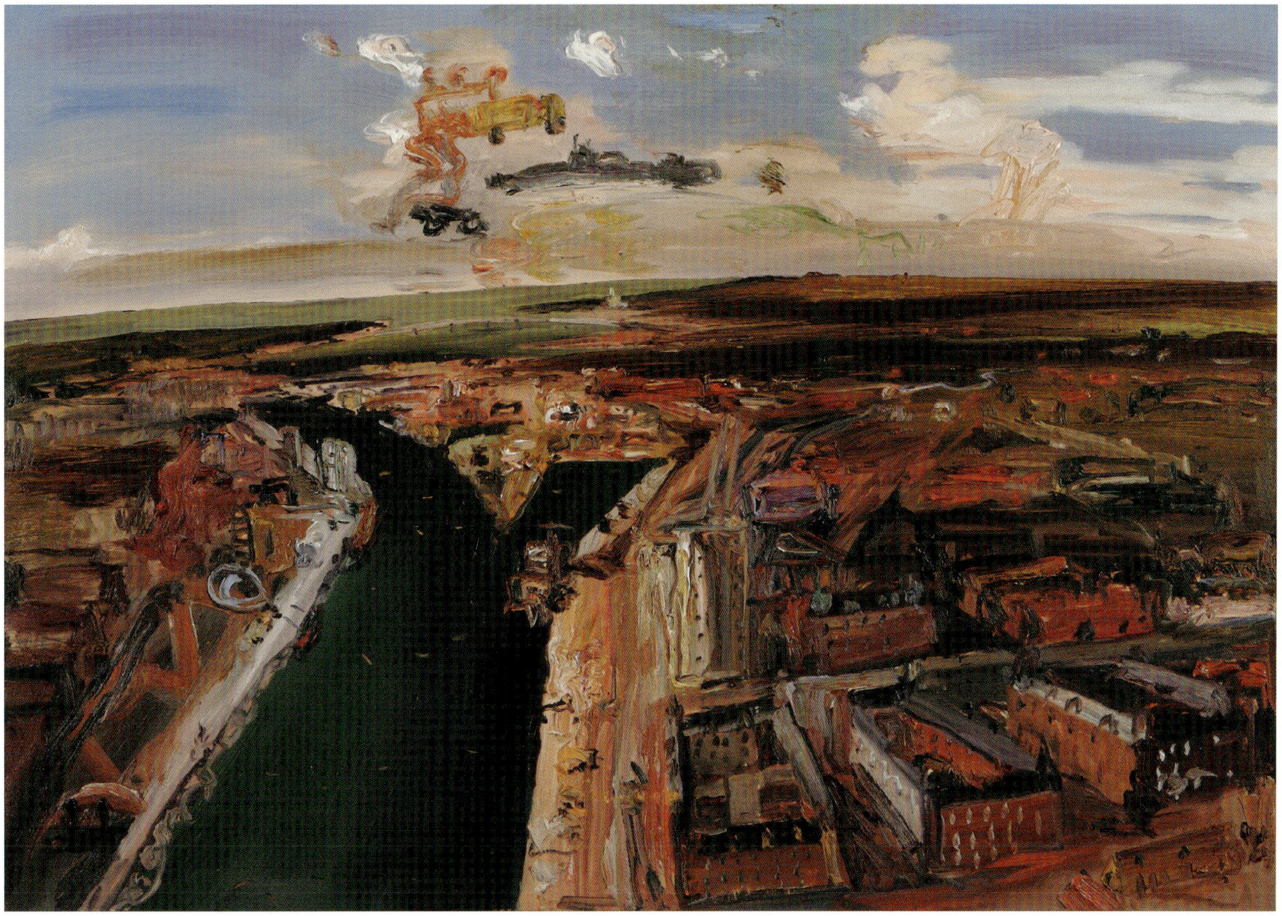

Fig. 2 John Hartman, *KobenHavn—Western Approach*, 1997, oil on linen, 76 x 107 cm (30 x 42 inches).

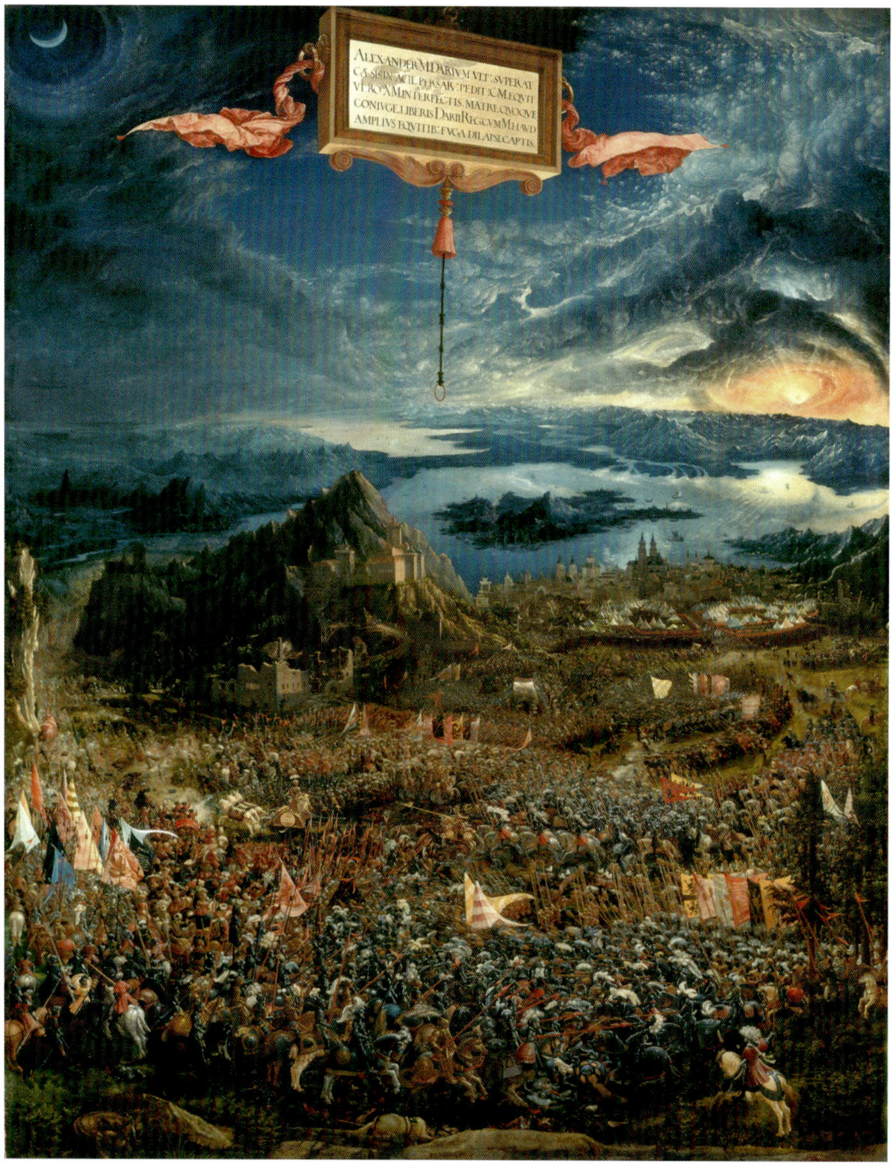

Fig. 3 Albrecht Altdorfer (1480–1538), *The Battle of Issus*, 1529, oil on limewood, 158.4 x 120.3 cm (62.4 x 47.4 inches). Alte Pinakothek, Munich, Bayerische Staatsgemäldesammlungen

high buildings. The city poses challenges for the painter, who is also a cartographer of sorts: he can observe the city in myriad ways, but must construct a holistic view from down on the street. As Hartman writes, "At ground level the city is visceral—all smell and sound and movement. I began to see New York as a pulsing body, its roads as arteries, its buildings as an armoured skin, the moving water and sky as a breathing lung, an open space of intense light."[3] The city becomes an extended analogy for "being" itself, forcing us to feel the limits of corporeal perception.

If the city is a body, Hartman paints it as such: the river becomes an intestinal tract taking care of all essential functions: cleansing, expelling, transporting, and cooling. The bridges, roads, streets, and highways ensure healthy circulation. The buildings and towers are the power centres, the processing plants—their greatest concentration is downtown, in the so-called "heart" of the city. The city consumes and expels incessantly—the guts of the corporeal being spill haphazardly over the landscape. Hartman's palette consists of a visceral range of sensuously applied bloody reds, fecal browns, and fleshy pinks.

With no desire to mask the muckiness of paint with hard lines or thin glazes, Hartman revels in letting the nature of the material inform the subject. He uses the three-dimensional properties of thick paint to build an intricate topographic surface that includes smoky areas of retreat where paint marks have been lifted off; their banishment is evident in the trail of the brush. In the painting *The Thames Looking West From Above Tower Bridge* (p. 117), Hartman has used perspective and atmosphere to construct a dramatic illusionistic space depicting a complex of bridges and buildings. The composition, however, is in danger of being upstaged by the paint: the viewer's eye is drawn to the intricately worked terrain of blobs, clumps, and smears comprising the skin of the work. Hartman maintains a precise balance between illusion and surface so that one does not lessen the impact of the other.

He is not interested in depicting the architectural grandeur of the city. His vision is much more a physical mapping-out of space, almost as if the details are secondary. Hartman feels his way through the city and these paintings aspire more toward a feeling of space occupied, of surrounding denseness. While referencing the sublime through his awesome panoramas, Hartman's gutsy translation of his subjects into a network of marks and colours creates its own agitated hum. The city becomes ecstatic, exalted, coaxing out a frenzy of sensory reactions. Still, Hartman's cityscapes enshrine the normal moment: this is any day without event. Of course, certain recent world events are inescapable and invite comparison with the destruction of Jericho. Seeing the foot of Manhattan Island denuded of the imposing forms of the Twin Towers will provoke specific memories for most viewers; Hartman shows us how cities hold memories, sustain tragedies, and heal themselves, adapting history into their very construction.

Hartman has cited Albrecht Altdorfer's (1480–1538) painting *The Battle of Issus* (1529) (fig. 3) as a seminal influence.[4] This work shows us a mind-stretching panorama seen from a bird's-eye view high above the ground. It depicts the preparations for a massive battle: countless soldiers and horses in the foreground, castles and ships in the middle ground. In the far distance, the painting sweeps back to show open waters and vast mountains at the edge of the horizon. All the elements in the painting—land, mountains, sky, sea, and human figures—seem to be surging together like waves on a rough sea. In his book *Landscape and Memory*, Simon Schama describes how this painting alters the landscape to reflect the story that is being told: "the apocalyptic defeat of the Persian king Darius by Alexander is not only registered in the magnitude of the brutal mountain that looms over the fray, but extended into the heavens, where the contours of the rocks are echoed in the swirling cloud forms."[5] Like Altdorfer, Hartman imbues his paintings with an underlying motion, injecting emotion into the landscape.

Hartman's massive painting *Halifax* (pp. 52–53) alludes to a cataclysmic event that happened almost one hundred

3 John Hartman, invitation to the exhibition "Rivers and Cities," held at Nicholas Metivier Gallery, October 27 to November 26, 2005.

4 Blodgett and Spalding, *Painting the Bay*, 13, 16.

5 Schama, *Landscape and Memory*, 426. Schama also refers his reader to Christopher S. Wood, *Albrecht Altdorfer and the Origins of Landscape* (Chicago: University of Chicago Press, 1993), 22.

years ago but rumbles down the century to the present day. The city of Halifax is seen in this triptych from the Dartmouth side of the Narrows; we see the harbour entrance on the left, the MacKay Bridge on the right, and the Bedford Basin beyond. The artist bends the two shorelines of Halifax to encompass the whole city in his rectangular picture frame. The conical cloud shape in the centre of the middle panel represents the Halifax Explosion, which occurred on December sixth, 1917, when the *Mont-Blanc*, a French merchant ship loaded with explosives, collided with a Norwegian steamship, the *Imo*. The ensuing explosion razed much of the city. Hartman has painted the ghosts of the two ships in the Narrows, close to the spot where they would have collided.

The conical cloud solves a compositional problem for Hartman in that it caps a triangular pattern implied by red arteries that cross the bridges and point to the summit of the cloud. It reinforces the tight, unnatural reshaping of the shoreline of the city; it is as if the two shores are reeling back from the force of the blast. The incendiary red that features in the central part of the composition corresponds to the area of the city that would have burned. The composition radiates out from the site of the explosion in concentric bands, with the highways and streets echoing the physical reverberations of 1917 in a ripple effect. Blood red is predominant in the painting's palette—it feels raw, as if alluding to a wound the city still bears.

Hartman has also woven a bit of personal history into *Halifax*. His father worked in the engine room of a corvette (a small, manoeuvrable, lightly armed warship, smaller than a frigate but larger than a coastal patrol craft) while in the navy during the Second World War. Hartman took photographs of the boiler room of a corvette (now a museum ship) parked in Halifax Harbour and, from these images, painted the scene into the voluminous triangular cloud that dominates the work. The boiler-room scene seems to search to make sense of the mechanics of the explosion, bringing the devastating event down to human scale: a place where ordinary people would have been working when it occurred. In so doing, Hartman embeds both private and public memory into his present-day vision of the city.

Hartman prepares for his city paintings with much contemplative study, reading, research, and rumination. He gathers together a plethora of visual sources—maps, books about the city, watercolour sketches and drawings done on-site, his own photographs, and historical documentation—before he begins to plan the painting. He seeks to strike a balance between faithful representation and the urge to create an aesthetically refined and rigorous composition. His experimentation with composition is evident in the preparatory works that can be seen in the sketchbooks included in this exhibition. Striving for a dynamic visual balance, he alters or morphs a given view to suit his pictorial objectives. Pencil sketches map the composition; watercolours provide colour and light. The sketchbooks include many variations on a particular view. These trial runs, along with supporting photographs, postcards, maps, and other source materials, serve as visual references when the time comes to manifest his vision in paint.

When beginning a painting, Hartman's first step is to rough in a drawing in red paint, forming a skeletal depiction of what is to come, what is to be built. He applies paint quickly, often working wet into wet paint, pushing and drawing into the thick globs of vibrant colour with athletic, expressive brushwork. An area of particularly heavy impasto may designate a place of significance in Hartman's mental mapping of the city or indicate a specific memory or event. Although he refers to photographs and preparatory studies while working, the urgent, energetic execution of the paintings seems a response more to subjective memory than to studied observation.

Hartman's paintings of cities and rivers invoke the eighteenth-century concept of the picturesque as set out by the theorists Uvedale Price, William Gilpin, and Richard Payne Knight. As Johanne Lamoureux writes, "the picturesque strives to compose tableaux independently of what is cited, and the ambition of the picturesque garden

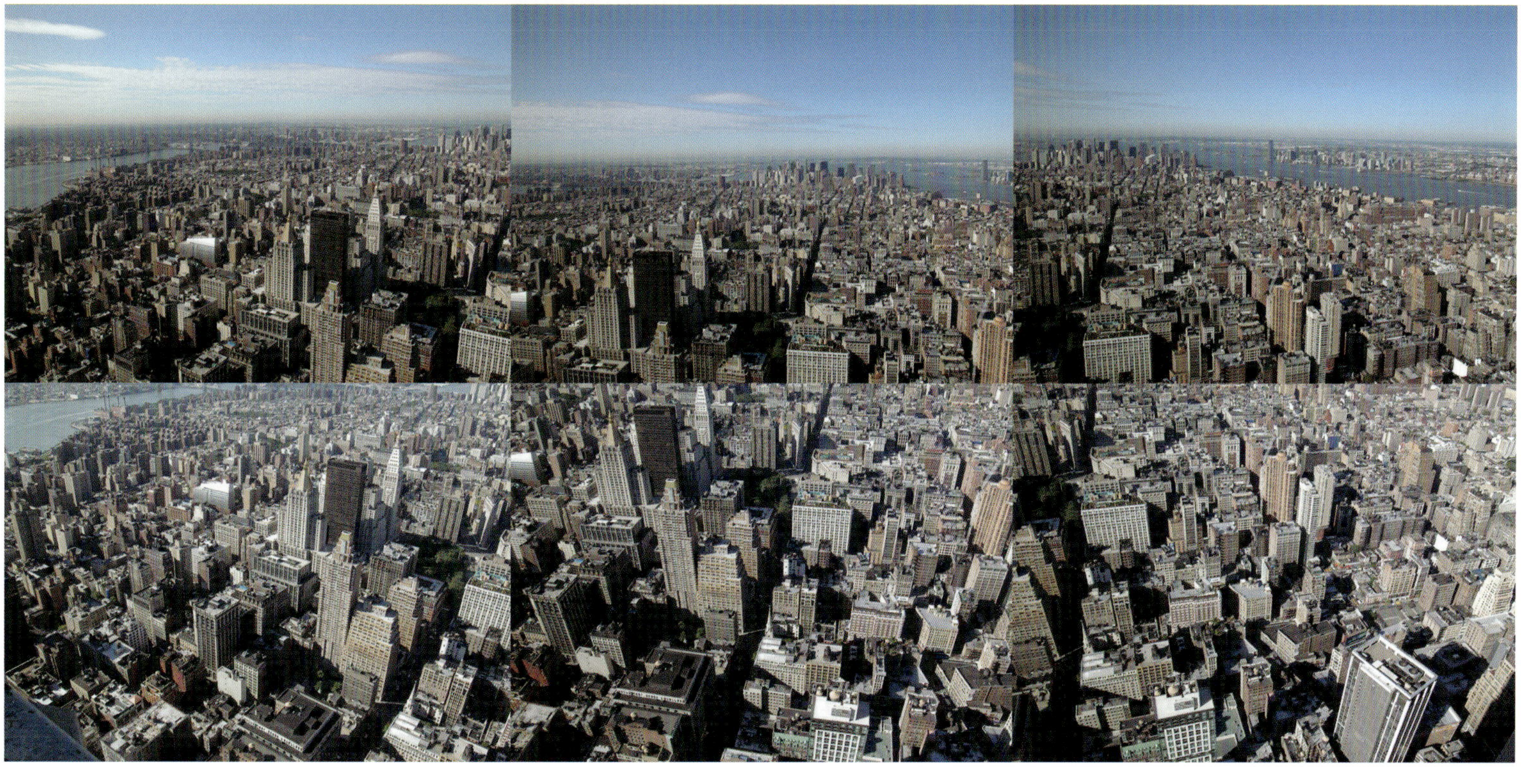

Fig. 4 John Hartman, digital photographs of Lower Manhattan from the Empire State Building, 2006.

is ideally to hold these separate pictures together."[6] However, Hartman avoids encumbering his compositions with details—the small flourishes that aspire to beauty—and also avoids focusing on particular natural phenomena that may connote the transcendence we associate with the sublime. The ambition of Hartman's city is to make fractured experience into a new whole. The artist's vision morphs the veracity of photographs and other sources into an altered panorama in which beauty, balance, and colour contribute to a dynamism that is more akin to the artist's experience of the place.

Hartman employs the principles of the picturesque in that he unifies disparate views, folding together different vantage points to realize his intended composition. In *Lower Manhattan* (pp. 100–101), Manhattan is indeed a picturesque garden. The foreground features buildings and streets seen from the perspective of the observatory of the Empire State Building, but toward Chelsea and the Financial District, the vantage point swings to a much higher level, a perspective available only from a plane flying over the scene. There is a seamless transition between the two viewpoints in that the painting does not rely on an exact replication of the city's grid, but instead grandly sweeps over the topography, the bustling motion of the city and the harbour, and the play of light over all of it. The artist wanted the composition to take on the tension of an incredibly dense triangle within a square in which the tip of Lower Manhattan points up like the prow of a ship. Working from a series of six photographs (fig. 4) joined together in a computer program, he manipulated the view, pulling the East River and the Hudson River down into the composition, pushing the viewpoint to a greater altitude. Therefore, the buildings in the foreground remain a substantial size, rather than being the tiny shapes in the original photographs.

Years ago, an artist friend showed Hartman a book of Oskar Kokoschka's paintings of aerial views of cities, and it made a lasting impression on him. As Hartman says, "Those paintings lodged into some compartment in my brain. I would be in a city and think that it would be interesting to paint it but have no idea how I would do it. I would go back to those Kokoschka paintings and remember them."[7] Kokoschka has been thought of as one of the great painters of the twentieth century, particularly for his revolutionary ability to make manifest his inner life and experiences in paint. Hartman also admires other European Expressionist painters, particularly Georges Rouault (1871–1958), Chaim Soutine (1893–1943), and Emil Nolde (1867–1956), who were exceptionally capable of expressing the conflicted anguish of the modern predicament in their painting style and subject matter.[8] Hartman's dynamic and athletic approach pays homage to his forebears' influence, but is rooted in an effort to probe contemporary ways of seeing.

It is interesting to compare Hartman's paintings of London, such as *The Thames Looking West From Above Tower Bridge* (p. 117), with Kokoschka's 1959 *View of the Thames* (fig. 5). (Kokoschka painted the Thames many times between 1925 and the 1970s, as well as river scenes in Prague, Lyon, Dresden, and Salzburg.) The two works share similar perspectives and scale in their views of the city. Although there are divergent colour sensibilities and definite differences in the mark-making between the two works, there is a kinship in terms of their visual rhythm and the dynamism of the overall surface. Both artists have translated the image to the canvas in a spontaneous, immediate manner.

The rivers and waterways in Hartman's paintings create a tension between concreteness and fluidity, between static and flowing. The intense coiling network of the city is often offset by blue vistas of sky and water that Hartman calls a sudden "hope of breathing,"[9] a more relaxed space than the city itself. Many cities were built around rivers—the original highways, routes for transport of goods and people—that still form the natural boundaries that define their shape. In many of the cities depicted by Hartman, we see the bridges, ferries, ships, docks, and port industry on which the city relies. Nowhere is this more evident than in

[6] Lamoureux, "Places and Commonplaces of the Picturesque," in *Sightlines: Reading Contemporary Canadian Art*, 297.
[7] John Hartman, interview with author, June 2006.
[8] Ness, *with minimal means*, 4.
[9] John Hartman, interview with author, summer 2006.

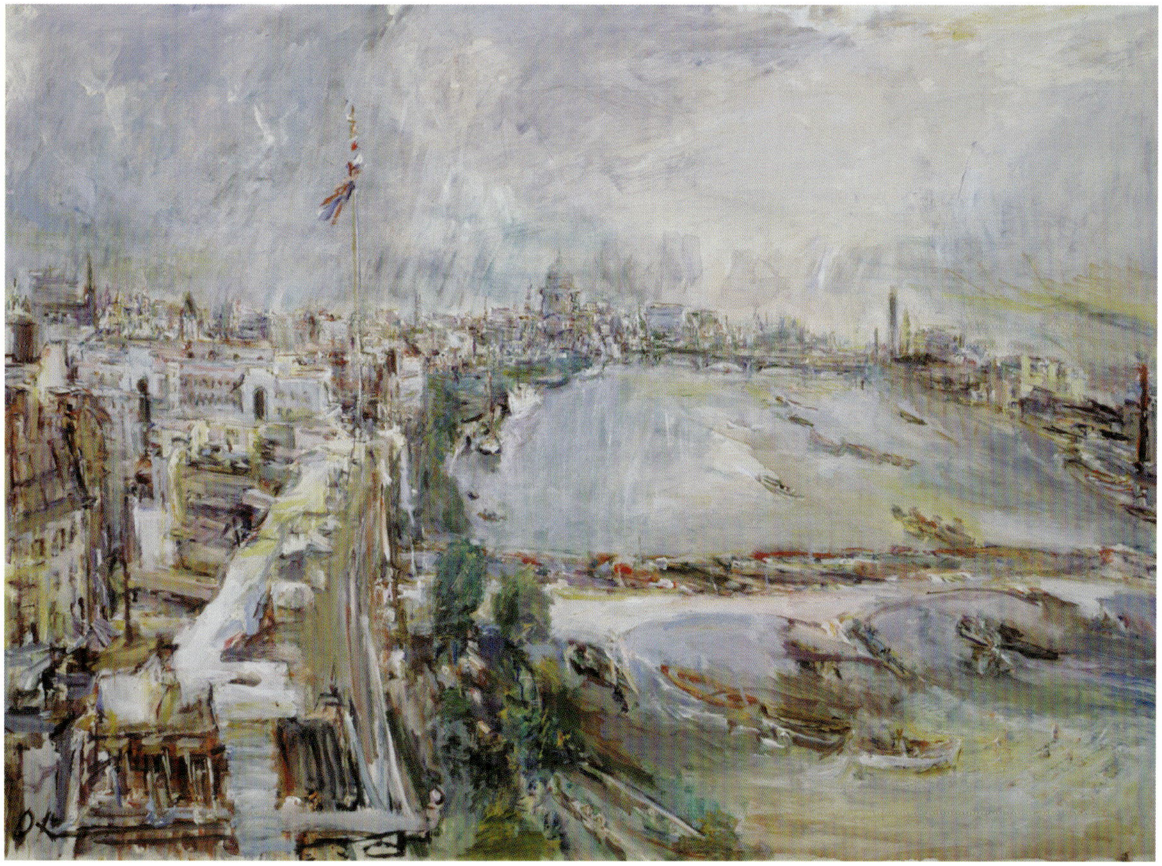

Fig. 5 Oskar Kokoschka (1886–1980), *View of the Thames*, 1959, oil on canvas, 91.4 x 123.2 cm (36 x 48.5 inches). Tate Gallery, London. © Art Resource, New York.

his paintings of London: the Thames appears as a vital thoroughfare, the crucial point of orientation in any conceptual rendering of the city.

In some of Hartman's city paintings, bodies of water also show the toxic effects of urban life. In the diptych *New York* (pp. 92–93), the Hudson River, in the lower right corner of the painting, is scumbled in dark orange and even a deep fiery red—perhaps an industrial spill, or other noxious effluents. Whatever the reason, the emotional, hot colours seem out of place, more suggestive of bodily fluids than a river.

The contemporary notion of virtual space has created a consciousness of being connected with other places and realities without physical contact. We can be everywhere at once with telephone lines, Web cams, television images, radio waves, and virtual realities. Technology provides the new bridges, roads, and pathways in the present-day cityscape. Hartman's paintings reflect this by embodying speed and synchronicity: in *Hamilton Harbour From Above* (p. 69), the city becomes like a piece of circuit board. The wharfs, docks, and slips of the harbour turn the natural curves of the shoreline into jutting rectangles. The simple geometry of the city plan looks much like the regimented grids that live inside our smart machines.

Line plays an important role in Hartman's paintings. He draws in the paint, rendering quick mental pictures that are not fully formed or modelled. The figurations are sketchy, yet remarkably eloquent. In his painting of a cold and wintry *Montreal* (p. 89), Hartman uses a shiver of loose, quick lines and tentative staccato marks to suggest the apparition of the city as seen from an imaginary vantage point high above Mount Royal. The downtown area becomes a dark huddle of forms, a warm heart within a broad expanse of white snow that is edged by the cool blue of the St. Lawrence River. This rendering of Montreal gives the viewer a sense of the artist's hand, his playful calligraphic style with the brush. While some of the other cities feel more solid, fully formed, *Montreal* is one of the loosest paintings in the series, hovering out of focus—content in its semi-abstraction.

Hartman's colleague and fellow painter David Urban has written: "Paintings exist in our minds as much as they exist on the wall or easel in front of us. So it follows that they may be thought of as imaginary or mental constructs that borrow reality in order to exist."[10] Paintings like *Montreal* show that Hartman has used cities as an imaginary construct to rattle our hold on perception. It does not matter if the painting looks like Montreal or not. As Urban points out, one can go further and say that the painting doesn't really need to hinge itself to the concept of Montreal at all, but is merely a painting for painting's sake, active in the mind of the viewer as a manifestation of the artist's vision. The viewer connects with the energy used to push the painting into existence. Leaving the big questions open and connecting with that intensity is what these paintings are all about.

John Hartman's paintings of cities unsettle our traditional ways of seeing because they are only loosely tethered to traditional concepts of realism. He takes traditional postcard-like vistas into new dreamlike territory, mapping out cityscapes that we feel intuitively as much as recognize visually. The influential German philosopher G. W. Leibniz (1646–1716) once wrote to a friend:

> *Vision seems to adapt itself to its object like the images that one has of a town when one contemplates it from the height of a tower; hearing is analogous to a view taken from outside and on the same level as the town; touch, finally, relates to (the understanding) of whoever comes in contact with a town from close up by wandering through its streets.*[11]

Leibniz describes the hierarchy of the senses in relation to experience in a way that is relevant to Hartman's painting strategy: he relies more on the sensual qualities of his chosen material than on the traditional visual means of representing place in painted form. His desire is not to replicate what he sees, but to create something new.

---

[10] Urban, "Painting's Radiant Array," *Border Crossings* 23, no. 3 (August 2004): 45.
[11] Leibniz, G. W., quoted in Vidler, *Warped Space*

Conceptually, Hartman's city paintings occupy a zone between the artist's experience of his subject and his aesthetic intention—the urge to create a good painting and all the choices that entails. Hartman's paintings amalgamate personal experience, recorded history, and a kaleidoscopic array of visual sources. From a lofty aerial perspective, they propose landscapes not unlike any other that Hartman has painted, drawing on memories that flicker in and out of focus and ambiguous images situated somewhere between motion and stillness, dream and reality, abstraction and representation. Hartman's cities are memory-mappings, apparitions of colour and form that are amorphous and compelling. The paintings as finished objects propose another duality: they exist both as images that carry all kinds of intellectual connotations—cities as ideas of cities—and as paintings that prompt a physical understanding of urban space through the body and all its senses.

STUART REID is the Director and Curator of the Tom Thomson Art Gallery in Owen Sound, Ontario.

Thanks to Jennifer Rudder, David Sereda and Lorissa Sengara for editing and proofreading, and to the Tom Thomson Art Gallery for support in research and writing of this text.

BIBLIOGRAPHY

Benjamin, Walter. *Illuminations*. Edited by Hannah Arendt. New York: Schocken Books, 1969.
Blodgett, Jean, and Jeffrey Spalding. *Painting the Bay: Recent Work by John Hartman*. Kleinburg, ON: McMichael Canadian Art Collection, 1993.
Danto, Arthur C. *After the End of Art: Contemporary Art and the Pale of History*. Princeton, NJ: Princeton University Press, 1997.
Dompierre, Louise, and Janine Marchessault. *Digital Gardens: A World in Mutation*. Toronto: The Power Plant, 1996.
Elkins, James. *Pictures & Tears: A History of People Who Have Cried in Front of Paintings*. New York: Routledge, 2001.
Hart, Matthew. *Big North: The Paintings of John Hartman*. Toronto: Key Porter Books, 1999.
Lamoureux, Johanne. "Places and Commonplaces of the Picturesque." In *Sightlines: Reading Contemporary Canadian Art*. Edited by Jessica Bradley and Lesley Johnstone. Montreal: Artextes Editions, 1994.
Ness, Kim. *with minimal means: John Hartman Prints, 1985–1995*. Hamilton: McMaster Museum of Art, 1995.
Olivares, Rosa, ed. *EXIT—Image & Culture*, no. 17. Madrid: Olivares & Associates Publishing, 2005.
Schama, Simon. *Landscape and Memory*. New York: Vintage Books, 1995.
Silcox, David P. *Painting Place: The Life and Work of David B. Milne*. Toronto: University of Toronto Press, 1996.
Urban, David. "Painting's Radiant Array." *Border Crossings* 23, no. 3 (August 2004).
Vidler, Anthony. *Warped Space: Art, Architecture, and Anxiety in Modern Culture*. Cambridge, MA: Massachusetts Institute of Technology, 2000.

BIOGRAPHY

JOHN HARTMAN

Born 1950, Midland, Ontario

EDUCATION

1973
Bachelor of Arts, McMaster University, Hamilton

SELECTED SOLO EXHIBITIONS

2007–2009
CITIES: John Hartman, curated by Stuart Reid, and circulated by the Tom Thomson Art Gallery, Owen Sound with the assistance of the Art Gallery of Nova Scotia to the Art Gallery of Nova Scotia, Halifax; Tom Thomson Art Gallery, Owen Sound; Art Gallery of Calgary, Calgary; Southern Alberta Art Gallery, Lethbridge; University of Toronto Art Centre, Toronto; Kenderdine Art Gallery, Saskatoon; Gallery Stratford, Stratford; MacLaren Art Centre, Barrie; Sir Wilfred Grenfell College Art Gallery, Corner Brook; The Rooms Provincial Art Gallery, St. John's

2007
CITIES, Jill George Gallery, London, England
CITIES, Charles Cowle Gallery, New York, USA
CITIES, Art 45, Montreal
CITIES, Nicholas Metivier Gallery, Toronto

2006
John Hartman: Watercolours and Drypoints, Paul Kuhn Gallery, Calgary

2005
Rivers and Cities, Nicholas Metivier Gallery, Toronto
John Hartman: Paintings, Watercolours and Prints of London, Scotland and Canada, Jill George Gallery, London, England
John Hartman: New Works, Paul Kuhn Gallery, Calgary

2004
John Hartman: Harbours—New Paintings, Pastels and Drypoints, Mira Godard Gallery, Toronto

2003
John Hartman: Recent Works, Paul Kuhn Gallery, Calgary

2002
John Hartman: From the Garden—New Works on Paper, Mira Godard Gallery, Toronto

2001
John Hartman: Georgian Bay and Newfoundland, Mira Godard Gallery, Toronto

2000
John Hartman: Recent Work, Paul Kuhn Gallery, Calgary

1999–2001
Big North: The Paintings of John Hartman, curated by Brian Meehan and circulated by the Tom Thomson Art Gallery and London Regional Art and Historical Museums to the Museum of Contemporary Canadian

Art, Toronto; Tom Thomson Memorial Art Gallery, Owen Sound; Kelowna Art Gallery, Kelowna; Mendel Art Gallery, Saskatoon; Nickle Arts Museum, Calgary; Art Gallery of Newfoundland and Labrador, St. John's; London Regional Art and Historical Museums, London

1999
John Hartman: New Paintings, Hart Gallery, London, England
John Hartman: New Paintings and Pastels, Mira Godard Gallery, Toronto

1998
The Artist's Garden, Mira Godard Gallery, Toronto
Panorama, Galerie Leif Jensen, Copenhagen, Denmark
Stories from the Northland, University of Lethbridge Art Gallery, Lethbridge

1997
John Hartman, Hart Gallery, London, England
John Hartman: New Work, Mira Godard Gallery, Toronto

1996
John Hartman: Recent Paintings, W. K. P. Kennedy Gallery, North Bay

1995–1997
with minimal means: John Hartman Prints, 1985–1995, curated by Kim Ness and circulated by the McMaster Museum of Art, to the Art Gallery of Newfoundland and Labrador, St. John's, Tom Thomson Memorial Art Gallery, Owen Sound; Laurentian University Museum and Art Centre, Sudbury; Art Gallery of Windsor, Windsor; University of Waterloo Art Gallery, Waterloo; Carleton University Art Gallery, Ottawa; McMaster Museum of Art, Hamilton

1995
Canadier i Kobenhavn, Galerie Leif Jensen, Copenhagen, Denmark
John Hartman: The Prints, Mira Godard Gallery, Toronto
John Hartman: New Work, Hart Gallery, London, England
Mount of Paradise, Mira Godard Gallery, Toronto
The Wrecking of the Midland Simcoe Elevator, Huronia Museum and Gallery of Art, Midland

1994
John Hartman, Buschlen Mowatt Gallery, Vancouver

1993
Painting the Bay: Recent Work by John Hartman, McMichael Canadian Art Collection, Kleinburg
John Hartman, olie, pastel, glas grafik, Galerie Ähuset, Koge, Denmark
John Hartman: öl auf Leinwand, Pastel, Lithographie, Galerie Schröder und Dörr, Bergisch Gladbach, Germany
John Hartman: Recent Paintings, Canadian Art Galleries, Calgary
John Hartman: Narrative Landscapes, Mira Godard Gallery, Toronto

1992
Fired Light—The Glass Paintings of John Hartman from the Workshop of Lars Frese, Copenhagen, circulated by the London Regional Art and Historical Museums to the MacLaren Art Centre, Barrie

1991
Expulsion from Paradise: an Allegory, 49th Parallel, New York, USA
The Big Picture, Mira Godard Gallery, Toronto
John Hartman, drypoint, lithograph and pastel, Christina Parker Fine Arts, St. John's

1990
New Works on Paper, Mira Godard Gallery, Toronto
Recent Paintings, The Library and Gallery, Cambridge, circulated to the MacLaren Art Centre, Barrie
Landscape Implications, Lynnwood Arts Centre, Simcoe

1988
Invisible stories — a series of four one-person exhibitions, curated by Kim Moodie, Embassy Cultural House, London
John Hartman: Maleri, Galeri Marius, Copenhagen, Denmark
John Hartman: Nord Canada/Usynlige Historier, Galeri Marius, Copenhagen, Denmark
The North: Life on the Edge, Agnes Etherington Art Centre, Kingston
The North/Invisible Stories, Gadatsy Gallery, Toronto

1987
Job's Garden, Gadatsy Gallery, Toronto
Jacob's Ladder, Robertson Gallery, Ottawa

1986–1987
John Hartman—Colour drypoint engravings, circulated to Ring House Gallery, University of Alberta, Edmonton; La Galerie d'Art, Stewart Hall, Pointe Claire; SAW Gallery, Ottawa; Macdonald Stewart Art Centre, Guelph

1986
Return to Paradise, Gadatsy Gallery, Toronto

1985
Highway 69 drawings, Gadatsy Gallery, Toronto

1984
Recent Works, Gadatsy Gallery, Toronto
Paintings and works on paper, La Galerie Shayne, Montreal

1983
Peintures et oeuvres sur papier, La Galerie Shayne, Montreal
Wendake drawings, Gadatsy Gallery, Toronto
John Hartman—new paintings and drawings, Art Gallery of Hamilton, Hamilton

1979–1982
Gadatsy Gallery, Toronto

1972
John Hartman, Trinity College, University of Toronto, Toronto

SELECTED GROUP EXHIBITIONS

2006
Far and Wide: The Paintings of David Alexander and John Hartman, Art Gallery of Alberta, Edmonton
Into the Collection, Winnipeg Art Gallery, Winnipeg

2005
Towards The Spiritual in Canadian Art, Varley Art Gallery, Unionville

2004
Skies, Macdonald Stewart Art Centre, Guelph

2003
The Prints of Ed Bartram, John Hartman, J. C. Heywood, Mira Godard Gallery, Toronto
Re: Collection, Tom Thomson Memorial Art Gallery, Owen Sound
Certain Realities, Mira Godard Gallery, Toronto
Horti-Culture, James Baird Gallery, St. John's
Remembered Landscape, James Baird Gallery, St. John's
The AGNL and the RCA: A Survey, Art Gallery of Newfoundland and Labrador, St. John's
Einstein's Brain, McMaster Museum of Art, Hamilton

2001

Alignments: Contemporary Works from the Permanent Collection, Art Gallery of Windsor, Windsor

Contemporary Painting, Sculpture and Ceramics, curated by Hart Gallery at Phillips Auctioneers, Leeds, England

2000–2003

Two Nations: Works on Paper, circulated by Whitewater Gallery, North Bay, to various galleries in Ontario and Cuba

2000

Landscape and Memory, Mira Godard Gallery, Toronto

1999

The Painters' Newfoundland: Selections from the Pouch Cove Collection, Sir Wilfred Grenfell College Art Gallery, Corner Brook

1998

Gathered Into Earth: Contemporary Landscape Painting, Sheehan Gallery, Walla Walla

The Painters' Newfoundland, Art Gallery of Newfoundland and Labrador, St. John's

Prints by Painters, Paul Kuhn Gallery, Calgary

1997

In Situ: Contemporary Canadian Prints, McMullen Gallery, University of Alberta, Edmonton

Nature Machine, Macdonald Stewart Art Centre, Guelph

1996–1997

Rediscovering the Landscape of the Americas, curated by Alan Gussow and circulated by the Gerald Peters Gallery, Santa Fe, USA, to Art Museum of South Texas, Corpus Christi, Texas, USA; Western Gallery, Western Washington University, Bellingham, Washington, USA; Memorial Art Gallery at the University of Rochester, Rochester, New York, USA; Gibbes Museum of Art, Charleston, South Carolina, USA

1996

Imagining Eden, curated by Tim Nowlin, Kenderdine Gallery, Saskatoon

Art 96, Hart Gallery, London, England

Beyond the Group of Seven, Heffel Gallery, Vancouver

Recent Acquisitions, Tom Thomson Memorial Art Gallery, Owen Sound

1995

Selected Works from the Collection of Daniel Donovan, Art Gallery of Hamilton, Hamilton

1994

Return to Paradise: Contemporary Views of Land by Canadian Artists, Edmonton Art Gallery, Edmonton

Reflecting Paradise, Howe Oil Tower, Calgary

John Hartman, Dan Hudson, Tim Zuck: Recent Works, West Parry Sound District Museum, Parry Sound

Contemporary Canadian Works from the Collection of the Art Gallery of the University of Lethbridge, curated by Glenn Cumming, Ford Centre for the Performing Arts, North York

A Public Responsibility: The OMERS Collection, Tom Thomson Memorial Art Gallery, Owen Sound

Hidden Values, Canadian Corporations Collect, McMichael Canadian Art Collection, Kleinburg, Ontario

1993

Reflecting Paradise, circulated by Lotte Gallery, Seoul, South Korea, to Dong Ah Gallery, Teagu, South Korea; KBS, Pusan, South Korea; Nam Do Cultural Centre, Kwangju, South Korea

Abstraction: Which Way From Here? curated by Jeffrey Spalding, Canada Trust Tower, Calgary

FIAC Edition, Editions Copenhagen and Grand Palais, Paris, France

Art Multiple, Editions Copenhagen, Dusseldorf, Germany

1992

Legal Perspective, McMichael Canadian Art Collection, Kleinburg

The Georgian Bay Experience, curated by Eve Baxter, Tom Thomson Memorial Art Gallery, Owen Sound

1990

Notes from Eden, Tom Thomson Memorial Gallery, Owen Sound

1989

Hartman, Thauberger & de Niverville, Mira Godard Gallery, Toronto

Glaskunst og Billege, Holstebro Kunstmuseum, Holstebro, Denmark

1988

Glaskunst og Billege, Galeri Brandt, Fredensborg, Denmark

1987

Drawing Conclusions, John B. Aird Gallery, Toronto

Alumni exhibition, McMaster University Art Gallery, Hamilton

1984

Kanada, Maler um Midland, Kulturhaus, Wetzlar, West Germany

1983

Hagen, Hartman, Marchessault & Cullen, Gadatsy Gallery, Toronto

1982

Inscape—Outscape, McMaster University Art Gallery, Hamilton

1977

Larmand-Pirosko, Gibbon, Hartman, McMaster University Art Gallery, Hamilton

1974

Editions 1 exhibition, circulated by the Ontario Art Council to the Aggregation Gallery, Toronto, to Robert McLaughlin Gallery, Oshawa; Agnes Etherington Art Centre, Kingston; Wells Gallery, Ottawa

SELECTED PUBLIC COLLECTIONS

Agnes Etherington Art Centre, Kingston
Art Gallery of Ontario, Toronto
Art Gallery of Newfoundland and Labrador, St. John's
Art Gallery of Nova Scotia, Halifax
Art Gallery of Windsor, Windsor
British Museum, London, England
Canada Council Art Bank, Ottawa
Carleton University Art Gallery, Ottawa
Georgian College, Barrie
Huronia Museum and Art Gallery, Midland
Kenderdine Art Gallery, University of Saskatchewan, Saskatoon
La Galerie d'Art, Stewart Hall, Pointe Claire
Laurentian University Museum and Art Centre, Sudbury
Macdonald Stewart Art Centre, Guelph
MacLaren Art Centre, Barrie
Masterworks Foundation, Bermuda
McMaster University, Hamilton
McMichael Canadian Art Collection, Kleinburg
Mendel Art Gallery, Saskatoon
Museum London, London
National Library of Canada, Ottawa
Ring House Gallery, University of Alberta, Edmonton
Robert McLaughlin Gallery, Oshawa
Royal Library, Copenhagen, Denmark
Sir Wilfred Grenfell College Art Gallery, Corner Brook
Tom Thomson Memorial Art Gallery, Owen Sound
Thunder Bay Art Gallery, Thunder Bay
University of Calgary Library, Calgary
University of Lethbridge Art Gallery, Lethbridge
W. K. P. Kennedy Gallery, North Bay

SELECTED CORPORATE COLLECTIONS

Bank of Montreal
Blake, Cassels & Graydon
Bunting, Warburg Inc.
BPI Mutual Funds
Ciba Geigy
Davies, Ward, Phillips & Vineberg
Ernst & Young
Esso Resources Canada Limited
Gowling, Strathy & Henderson
Hewlett Packard
Household Financial Corporation Limited
Imperial Oil Limited
Lac Minerals
Lenczner, Slaght, Royce, Smith & Griffin
Maclean Hunter Ltd.
McCarthy Tétrault
McMillan Binch
Morris/Rose/Legett
Nesbitt Burns
Osler, Hoskin & Harcourt
Petro-Canada
Royal Bank of Canada
Scotiabank Group Fine Art Collection
Sun Life Assurance Company of Canada
SunLife Trust
Swiss Bank Corporation
Toronto-Dominion Bank
Torys LLP
Trimark Investments Management Inc.

SELECTED BIBLIOGRAPHY

Blodgett, Jean, and Jeffrey Spalding. *Painting The Bay: Recent Work by John Hartman*. Exhibition catalogue. McMichael Canadian Art Collection, Kleinburg, 1993.

Bodner, Debra, *Fired Light: The Fired Glass Paintings of John Hartman from the Workshop of Lars Frese, Copenhagen, Denmark*. Exhibition catalogue. Published on the occasion of the exhibition organized by the London Regional Art and Historical Museums, London. Canada: Hearn/Kelly Printing Co., 1992.

Brien, Peter. "I paint the land out of love." *The Globe and Mail* (September 25, 1999): C6.

Eyland, Cliff. "Painting Away." *Border Crossings* 67: 65–66.

Farr, Dorothy. *The North: Life on the Edge*. Kingston: Agnes Etherington Art Centre, 1988.

Hart, Matthew. *Big North: The Paintings of John Hartman*. Toronto: Key Porter Books, 1999.

Hart, Matthew. "Focus on John Hartman." *Canadian Art* 6, no. 3 (Fall 1989): 119.

Hart, Matthew. "Matthew Hart considers The Mission." *Canadian Art* 14, no. 1 (Spring 1997): 44–49.

Jordan, Betty Ann. "John Hartman at Mira Godard." *The Globe and Mail* (May 10, 1997).

MacKay, Gillian. "Conjuring a sense of awe." *The Globe and Mail* (July 15, 2000): R10.

MacKay, Gillian. "A Visual pilgrim's progress." *The Globe and Mail* (July 19, 1997): C12.

Milroy, Sarah. "The Great Canadian Printmaking Competition." *Canadian Art* (Spring 1995).

Moodie, Kim. *Invisible Stories*. Exhibition catalogue. London: Embassy Cultural House, 1988.

Ness, Kim. *with minimal means: John Hartman Prints, 1985–1995*. Exhibition catalogue. Hamilton: McMaster Museum of Art, 1995.

Spalding, Jeffrey. *Reflecting Paradise/ Reflets du Paradis*. Canadian Participation EXPO 1993, Taejon, South Korea, 1993.

Swain, Robert, and Robert Fulford. *Hidden Values*. Vancouver: Douglas and McIntyre, 1994.

Willard, Christopher. "John Hartman, Paul Kuhn Gallery." *Canadian Art* (Fall 2005): 148.

SELECTED PUBLICATIONS

Hartman, John, and Florence Vale. *A Couch of Grass*. Toronto: Five Publishers, 1993.

Hartman, John. *The Peaceable Kingdom of Gilbert Desrochers*. Kleinburg: McMichael Canadian Art Collection, 1991.

Hartman, John, and Barry Wilmont. *Pale Ports of Amber*. Toronto/Copenhagen, Denmark: Pavilion Neuf, 1991.

Hartman, John. *Georgian Bay*. Peterborough: Broadview Press, 1989.

Hartman, John, and Christine Boyanoski. *W. J. Wood: Paintings and Graphics*. Toronto: Art Gallery of Ontario, 1983.

Hartman, John. *Second Nature: An Exhibition of New Pastoral Art*. Barrie Gallery Project, 1988.

LIST OF WORKS

OIL ON LINEN

pp. 52–53
HALIFAX, 2006
244 x 503 cm (96 x 198 inches), triptych
Commissioned by Scotiabank Group as a gift to the
Art Gallery of Nova Scotia, Halifax
to commemorate the Bank's 175th anniversary

p. 55
THE NARROWS, 2006
152 x 168 cm (60 x 66 inches)
Collection of Scotiabank Group Fine Art Collection

pp. 58–59
VANCOUVER FROM ABOVE
BURRARD INLET, 2006
198 x 229 cm (78 x 90 inches)
Courtesy of Nicholas Metivier Gallery, Toronto

pp. 62–63
VANCOUVER, 2006
168 x 552 cm (66 x 172 inches), triptych
Collection of Andrew and Valerie Pringle

p. 65
BURRARD INLET, 2006
122 x 137 cm (48 x 54 inches)
Private Collection

p. 67
CALGARY, 2006
152 x 168 cm (60 x 66 inches)
Collection of Bennett Jones LLP, Toronto

p. 69
HAMILTON HARBOUR FROM ABOVE, 2004
152 x 168 cm (60 x 66 inches)
Collection of David and Robin Young

p. 73
PORT SEVERN, 2004
152 x 168 cm (60 x 66 inches)
Collection of John Wood and Debbie Daymond

p. 75
PARRY SOUND, 2003
203 x 196 cm (80 x 77 inches)
Collection of Sylvia and Jim McGovern

p. 79
OWEN SOUND, 2005
168 x 152 cm (66 x 60 inches)
Collection of Brian and Susan Lahey

p. 85
THE WESTERN CHANNEL, TORONTO, 2006
152 x 168 cm (60 x 66 inches)
Courtesy of Nicholas Metivier Gallery, Toronto

p. 87
TORONTO HARBOUR LOOKING EAST, 2005
117 x 132 cm (46 x 52 inches)
Collection of Andrew and Valerie Pringle

p. 89
MONTREAL, 2005
122 x 137 cm (48 x 54 inches)
Courtesy of Nicholas Metivier Gallery, Toronto

pp. 92–93
NEW YORK, 2005
251 x 335 cm (99 x 132 inches), diptych
Courtesy of Nicholas Metivier Gallery, Toronto

p. 95
MANHATTAN FROM ABOVE BROOKLYN, 2005
152 x 168 cm (60 x 66 inches)
Collection of Scotiabank Group Fine Art Collection

pp. 100–101
LOWER MANHATTAN, 2006
198 x 229 cm (78 x 90 inches)
Collection of Sylvia and Jim McGovern

p. 105
MANHATTAN AT NIGHT, 2006
152 x 168 cm (60 x 66 inches)
Collection of Robert and Tina Buchan

p. 107
THE SOUTHSIDE HILLS, ST. JOHN'S, 2004
122 x 137 cm (48 x 54 inches)
Courtesy of Nicholas Metivier Gallery, Toronto

p. 109
GLASGOW, 2004
122 x 137 cm (48 x 54 inches)
Collection of John Kelly and Stella McTernan

p. 115
THE THAMES FROM SWISS RE, 2005
152 x 168 cm (60 x 66 inches)
Collection of Richard Griffiths

p. 117
THE THAMES LOOKING WEST
FROM ABOVE TOWER BRIDGE, 2004
122 x 137 cm (48 x 54 inches)
Private Collection

SKETCHES AND WATERCOLOURS

All sketches and watercolours collection of the artist and courtesy of Nicholas Metivier Gallery unless otherwise noted

p. 18
STUDY FOR PORT SEVERN, 2004
Watercolour on paper
28.5 x 30 cm (11.25 x 12.75 inches)

pp. 22–23
HALIFAX FROM DARTMOUTH, 2006
Watercolour and graphite on paper; Concertina folding sketchbook 1, pp. 44–47, bound paper, 138 pages
24 x 17 cm (9.5 x 6.5 inches), folded

p. 24
TORONTO, 2005
Watercolour on paper
27 x 39 cm (10.5 x 15.25 inches)

pp. 50–51
HALIFAX, 2006
Pastel on paper
76 x 164 cm (30 x 64.5 inches), triptych

p. 57
BURRARD INLET, VANCOUVER
2006
Watercolour and graphite on paper; Concertina folding sketchbook 1, pp. 32–33, bound paper, 138 pages
24 x 17 cm (9.5 x 6.5 inches), folded

pp. 60–61
VANCOUVER, 2006
Watercolour and graphite on paper; Concertina folding sketchbook 1, pp. 2–5, bound paper, 138 pages
24 x 17 cm (9.5 x 6.5 inches), folded

p. 71
PORT SEVERN, 2004
Watercolour on paper
28.5 x 38 cm (11.25 x 15 inches)

pp. 76–77
OWEN SOUND HARBOUR, c. 1940 and WINTER BERTHS, OWEN SOUND, 2004
Ink on paper; Concertina folding sketchbook 4, pp. 60–63, bound paper, 138 pages
24 x 17 cm (9.5 x 6.5 inches), folded

p. 81
TORONTO LOOKING WEST, 2005
Watercolour and graphite on paper; Coptic bound sketchbook 3, pp. 181–182, bound paper, 280 pages
22 x 17 cm (8.5 x 6.5 inches), folded

p. 83
TORONTO FROM ABOVE THE HARBOUR LOOKING WEST, 2005
Watercolour on paper
28.5 x 30 cm (11.25 x 12 inches)

p. 90
EAST RIVER, MANHATTAN, 2005
Watercolour on paper
28.5 x 32 cm (11.25 x 12.5 inches)

p. 91
STUDY FOR NEW YORK, 2005
Watercolour on paper
29 x 34 cm (11.5 x 13.25 inches)

p. 96
VIEWS FROM THE EMPIRE STATE BUILDING, NEW YORK CITY, 2006
Graphite on paper; Concertina folding sketchbook 1, pp. 42–43, bound paper, 138 pages
24 x 17 cm (9.5 x 6.5 inches), folded

p. 97
LOWER MANHATTAN FROM THE EMPIRE STATE BUILDING, 2006
Watercolour and graphite on paper; Concertina folding sketchbook 1, pp. 40–41, bound paper, 138 pages
24 x 17 cm (9.5 x 6.5 inches), folded

p. 98
MANHATTAN, EAST RIVER, HUDSON RIVER
2005
Watercolour on paper
29 x 32 cm (11.25 x 12.5 inches)
Collection of Mark Kingwell

p. 99
MANHATTAN, 2005
Watercolour on paper
28.5 x 29 cm (11.25 x 11.5 inches)

p. 103
STUDY FOR MANHATTAN AT NIGHT, 2006
Watercolour and newspaper illustration on paper
28.5 x 32 cm (11.25 x 12.5 inches)

pp. 110–111
THE THAMES, 2004
Watercolour and graphite on paper; Concertina folding sketchbook 2, pp. 14–17, bound paper, 138 pages
24 x 17 cm (9.5 x 6.5 inches), folded

p. 113
THE THAMES RIVER FROM ABOVE WATERLOO BRIDGE, 2004
Pencil on paper; Concertina folding sketchbook 2, pp. 105–106, bound paper, 138 pages
24 x 17 cm (9.5 x 6.5 inches), folded

When I was a kid I always dreamed of flying.
I had this ability to imagine the ground as a film—the Earth as
a moving picture rolling towards me at an oblique angle.
Now, because I am able to gather the information, I can do that.

JOHN HARTMAN

ACKNOWLEDGEMENTS

JOHN HARTMAN

The *Cities* paintings began with a memory of how beautiful the industrial waterfront of Hamilton looked from the Burlington Skyway bridge. I soon discovered that making a painting of this memory required a great deal of walking, looking, sketching and taking photographs. Once I learned how the city looked up close I could imagine it and paint it from above.

This required faith on my part that all this might make a good painting and faith that this new direction my work was taking would be worthwhile. But this is what artists do and therefore not remarkable. What is remarkable to me is that at every turn, there were people who wanted to become part of the growing project, as this single painting led to many paintings, and then became an exhibition and a book. It is these people that I would like to acknowledge and thank for their belief in my art work.

Many of these paintings are in collections and I would like to thank the lenders, who, after liking the paintings enough that they wanted to acquire them and live with them, have been willing to turn around and give them up for two years, through the duration of the touring exhibit.

My wife Trish, has always believed in my work and been an ardent critic.

Nicholas Metivier saw early on that the *Cities* paintings formed a distinct body of work and has been unflagging in his efforts to bring the best people available into the project.

Stuart Reid at the Tom Thomson Art Gallery selected the show, organized the exhibition tour and took the time from a busy schedule to research and write about the artwork. Jeffrey Spalding, at the Art Gallery of Nova Scotia, has played a pivotal role in the *Cities* project.

Noah Richler has written insightfully about the paintings and now I think about my art work in ways I hadn't previously imagined. Dennis Reid provided a thoughtful preface that anchors this book to my early work and interest in the history of art in Canada.

My son Joseph made some wonderful large format photographs of me at work in the studio, not an easy task when the subject is telling you what to do.

Barr Gilmore's book design is an elegant response to the artwork and the writing. Amanda Sebris shepherded the design and publication, from gestation to reality, with a calm manner and a firm hand. Noel and David Saltmarche photographed the paintings and their perfectionism made the gorgeous reproductions in this book possible. Stephen Hutchings at Altitude Press has given the publication unqualified support.

Sarah Massie, Sarah Kennedy and Dionne MacAffee at the Nicholas Metivier Gallery; Sarah McMaster at the Tom Thomson Art Gallery; and Ray Cronin at the Art Gallery of Nova Scotia have all been generous with their time and I am grateful for their patience in dealing with a continuous stream of requests.

Scotiabank Group has been an early and a continuing supporter of my work through its collection, its past sponsorship of *Big North*, and its sponsorship of *Cities*. Finally I would like to acknowledge and thank Rick Waugh and Jane Nokes for making this book and exhibition a central part of Scotiabank Group's 175th celebrations.

Lafontaine, January 2007

Published on the occasion of the 175th anniversary of Scotiabank and the touring exhibition

CITIES JOHN HARTMAN

Design and typesetting by Barr Gilmore
Project management by Amanda Sebris

Edited by Lorissa Sengara, Amanda Sebris, and Norbert Sebris

All photography and digital colour work by See Spot Run Inc., Toronto, with the exception of the following: p. 118 by McMichael Canadian Art Collection; p. 121 by Simon Lautrop, Copenhagen; p.122 by Joachim Blavel – ARTOTHEK; Tate Gallery, London / Art Resource, NY (ART83458)

Documentary photography by Joseph Hartman (front/back endpapers, pp. 36–37), John Hartman (p. 28, 125), Noah Richler (pp. 34–35, 40–41) and Trish Hartman (pp. 46–47).

Travelling exhibition circulated by the Tom Thomson Art Gallery with the assistance of the Art Gallery of Nova Scotia to the Art Gallery of Nova Scotia, Halifax; Tom Thomson Art Gallery, Owen Sound; Art Gallery of Calgary, Calgary; Southern Alberta Art Gallery, Lethbridge; University of Toronto Art Centre, Toronto; Kenderdine Art Gallery, Saskatoon; Gallery Stratford, Stratford; MacLaren Art Centre, Barrie; Sir Wilfred Grenfell College Art Gallery, Corner Brook; The Rooms Provincial Art Gallery, St. John's.

Travelling exhibition organized by Nicholas Metivier Gallery, Toronto; Art 45, Montreal; Charles Cowles Gallery, New York, USA; and Jill George Gallery, London, England.

This catalogue was generously sponsored by

Scotiabank Group™ 175 YEARS

Published by Altitude Publishing, Canmore, Alberta

Altitude

Printed on Garda Silk and Mohawk Superfine in Canada by Friesens.

Library and Archives Canada Cataloguing in Publication

Harman, John, 1950-
Cities: John Hartman
contributing authors, Noah Richler, Stuart Reid, Dennis Reid ... [et al.]

Exhibition catalogue.
ISBN 978-1-55153-312-4

1. Hartman, John, 1950-. 2. Cities and towns in art. I. Richler, Noah. II. Reid, Stuart. III. Reid, Dennis. IV. Title.

ND249.H378A4 2007 759.11 C2007-900170-X

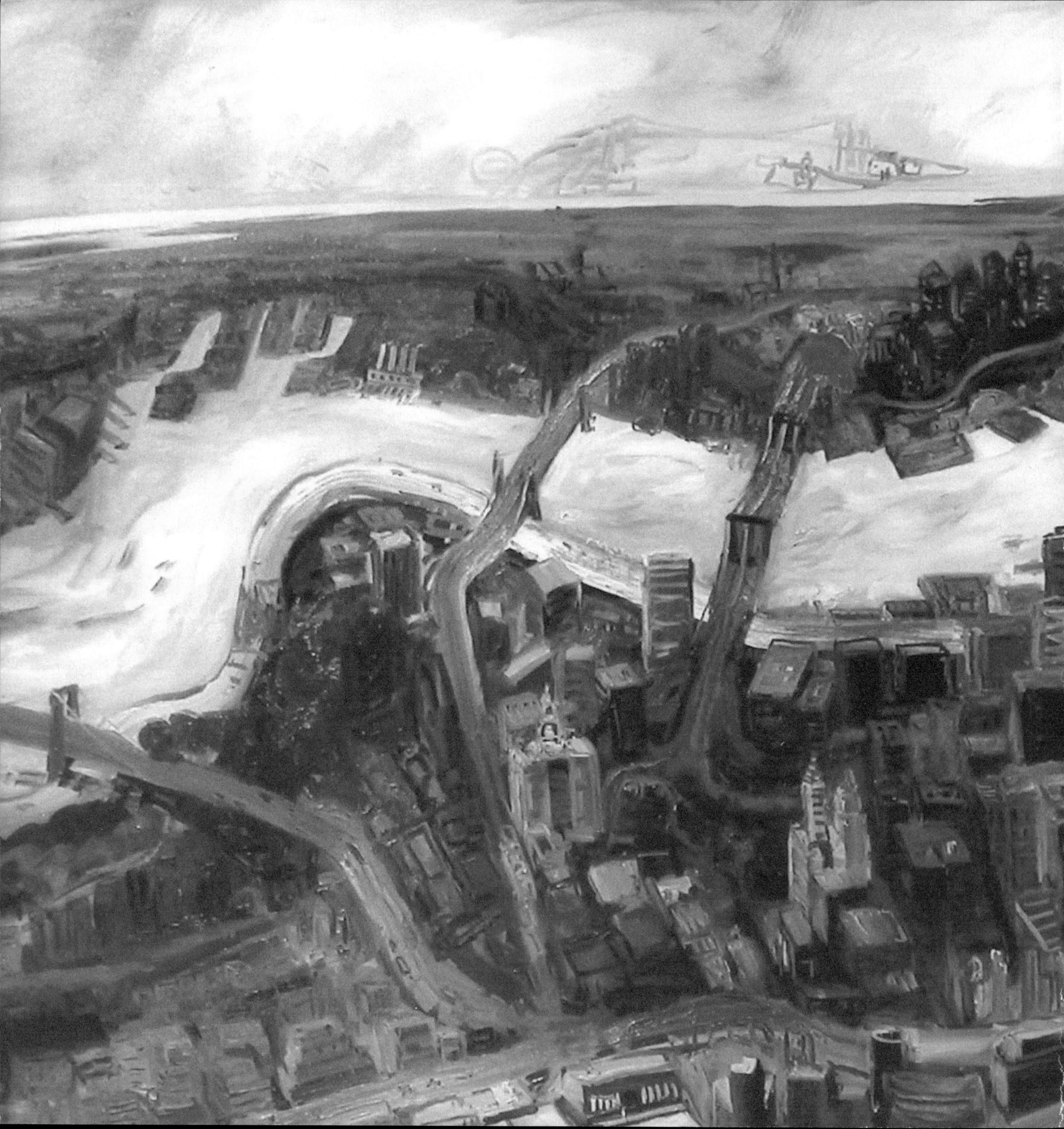